PRAISE FOR *THE PRAYER THAT TURNS THE WORLD UPSIDE DOWN*

"My friend Albert Mohler has given us a characteristically thoughtful and illuminating reflection on the magnificent prayer that Jesus himself taught us—a prayer that the entire Christian community prays together and which reminds us that we are all 'beggars at the throne of grace.'"

—Robert P. George, McCormick Professor of Jurisprudence, Princeton University

"Dr. Albert Mohler's insights never fail to amaze and enlighten. He is a gifted expositor with an uncanny ability to see and explain the big picture, yet with a keen eye for detail. His ability to distill complex theology in understandable language is unsurpassed. And all those qualities shine brightly in this book."

—Dr. John MacArthur, pastor of Grace Community Church and president of the Master's University and Seminary

"The Lord's Prayer is one of my favorite Scriptures. Albert Mohler is one of my favorite writers. This book is the result of the two coming together, and it will bless and encourage all who visit its pages."

—Daniel L. Akin, president, Southeastern Baptist Theological Seminary, Wake Forest, North Carolina

"We need a prayer revolution in the church and in America today. Faith and hope await each person who reads this exciting and robust book about how prayer turns the world upside down. It happened before and it can happen again. Let faith arise!"

—Dr. Ronnie Floyd, president, National Day of
Prayer; senior pastor, Cross Church

"Jesus taught his disciples to pray; Albert Mohler helps me see deeper into the meaning of the glorious truths Jesus taught. This book gives enlightenment and encouragement for life's journey."

—Dr. Johnny Hunt, senior pastor of FBC Woodstock;
former president of the Southern Baptist Convention

"A seminary president writing a book on prayer. Now that is novel! But this book is not about just any prayer. This is about our Lord's model prayer. And it is penned by an earnest practitioner of prayer who believes that seminaries and churches are radically changed by the practice or fervent prayer. For a guide to future fruitfulness, purchase this book. To be a recipient of the benedictions of our God, read and practice this volume."

—Paige Patterson, president, Southwestern Baptist
Theological Seminary, Fort Worth, Texas

"For atheists not in a foxhole, prayer is nonsense. For religious people, it is either a liturgical act or a private devotion. But in this fascinating study of the Lord's Prayer, Al Mohler shows how revolutionary genuine, radical, Gospel-focused prayer can be. Highly recommended!"

"Albert Mohler beautifully and brilliantly expounds on the biblical meaning and theological depth of the Lord's Prayer for twenty-first-century believers. Providing readers with thoughtful insights regarding the meaning and importance of prayer, as informed by scripture, theology, and church history, this readable and accessible volume invites readers to consider afresh the connection with and relationship between faithful prayers, kingdom-focused praise, the glory of God, and the gospel of grace. Church leaders and laypersons alike will be encouraged and challenged in their understanding of prayer, biblical piety, and theologically informed worship. Highly recommended!"

THE PRAYER THAT TURNS THE WORLD UPSIDE DOWN

THE LORD'S PRAYER AS A MANIFESTO FOR REVOLUTION

R. ALBERT MOHLER JR.

NELSON
BOOKS

An Imprint of Thomas Nelson

Published in Nashville, Tennessee, by Nelson Books, an imprint of Thomas Nelson. Nelson Books and Thomas Nelson are registered trademarks of HarperCollins Christian Publishing, Inc.

Published in association with the literary agency of Wolgemuth & Associates, Inc.

Thomas Nelson titles may be purchased in bulk for educational, business, fund-raising, or sales promotional use. For information, please e-mail SpecialMarkets@ThomasNelson.com.

Scripture quotations are taken from the ESV® Bible (The Holy Bible, English Standard Version®). Copyright © 2001 by Crossway, a publishing ministry of Good News Publishers. Used by permission. All rights reserved.

Italics in Scripture have been added by the author for emphasis.

ISBN 978-0-7180-9917-6 (eBook)
ISBN 978-0-7180-9093-7 (HC)
ISBN 978-1-4041-0758-8 (Custom)

Library of Congress Cataloging-in-Publication Data

Names: Mohler, R. Albert, Jr., 1959- author.
Title: The prayer that turns the world upside down : the Lord's Prayer as a manifesto for revolution / R. Albert Mohler Jr.
Description: Nashville : Thomas Nelson, 2018.
Identifiers: LCCN 2017013748 | ISBN 9780718090937
Subjects: LCSH: Lord's prayer.
Classification: LCC BV230 .M64 2018 | DDC 226.9/606--dc23 LC record available at https://lccn.loc.gov/2017013748

Printed in the United States of America

18 19 20 21 22 QG 10 9 8 7 6 5 4 3 2 1

Dedicated to
Benjamin Miller Barnes

Grandson of unspeakable joy. Who knew that one little boy could so utterly change the way I look at the world? May you grow to be a great man of God, worthy of your name, a faithful follower of Christ, and a light to your own generation.

In the meantime, just know that you make your parents so proud and your grandparents unbelievably happy. I love you even more than I knew I could.

Papa

REDISCOVER
THE POWER, BEAUTY, AND **LIFE-CHANGING** IMPACT OF THE **LORD'S PRAYER**

Take your congregation through a radical rediscovery of the Lord's Prayer: A prayer that turns the world upside down, toppling every earthly power and announcing God's reign over all things, in heaven and on earth.

The Lord's Prayer is one of the most powerful prayers in the Bible, taught by Jesus to his own disciples. This generation of Christians desperately needs to learn from Christ himself how we are to unleash the power and discipline of prayer.

This fall, teach your church how to participate in the radical, transformative prayer that Jesus taught his first disciples.

Go to **ChurchSource.com/LordsPrayer** to:
- **Save 65%** on cases and get **FREE shipping** with promo code **LORDSPRAYER**
- **FREE DOWNLOAD** study guide and sermon outlines

Fall 2018
Back-to-Church
Campaign

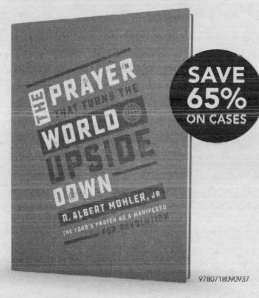

SAVE 65% ON CASES

THE PRAYER THAT TURNS THE WORLD UPSIDE DOWN

R. ALBERT MOHLER, JR.

THE LORD'S PRAYER AS A MANIFESTO FOR REVOLUTION

9780718090937

And when you pray, you must not be like the hypocrites. For they love to stand and pray in the synagogues and at the street corners, that they may be seen by others. Truly, I say to you, they have received their reward. But when you pray, go into your room and shut the door and pray to your Father who is in secret. And your Father who sees in secret will reward you.

And when you pray, do not heap up empty phrases as the Gentiles do, for they think that they will be heard for their many words. Do not be like them, for your Father knows what you need before you ask him. Pray then like this:

Our Father in heaven,
hallowed be your name.
Your kingdom come,
your will be done,
on earth as it is in heaven.
Give us this day our daily bread,
and forgive us our debts,
as we also have forgiven our debtors.
And lead us not into temptation,
but deliver us from evil.

CONTENTS

Introduction   xv

Chapter 1   The Lord's Prayer: An Overview   1

Chapter 2   And When You Pray: Why Jesus Doesn't
            Think Much of Routine Christian Prayer   17

Chapter 3   Hallowing the Father's Name: Where
            Authentic Prayer Begins   25

Chapter 4   Your Kingdom Come: Whose Agenda
            Is Our Concern Anyway?   47

Chapter 5   Give Us This Day: God's Abundant
            Physical Provisions   69

Chapter 6   Forgive Us Our Debts: The Prayer of
            God's New Covenant People   81

Chapter 7   Lead Us Not Into Temptation: Fighting
            the Enemy Through Prayer   95

Epilogue   Thine Is the Kingdom   111

Acknowledgments   119

Notes   121

About the Author   125

INTRODUCTION

We long for revolution. Something within us cries out that the world is horribly broken and must be fixed. For centuries, the word *revolution* was scarcely heard, buried under ages of oppression. The word itself was feared and speaking it was treason. And then, revolutions seemed to appear almost everywhere.

Some historians have gone so far as to identify our modern epoch as "The Age of Revolution." Is it? Perhaps it is more accurate to refer to our times as "The Age of Failed Revolution." Looking across the landscape, it becomes clear that very few revolutions produce what they promise. Arguably, most revolutions lead to a worse set of conditions than they replaced.

And yet, we still yearn for radical change, for things to be made right. We rightly long to see righteousness and truth and justice prevail. We are actually desperate for what no earthly revolution can produce. We long for the kingdom of God and for Jesus as King of kings and Lord of lords. We are looking for a kingdom that will never end and a King whose rule is perfect.

This is why Christians pray the Lord's Prayer. As we will see, this is the very prayer that Jesus taught his own disciples to pray. So Christians pray this prayer as a way of learning *how* to pray and *what* to pray—as Jesus teaches us to pray.

The Lord's Prayer is the prayer that turns the world upside down. Are you looking for revolution? There is no clearer call to revolution than when we pray "*Your* kingdom come, *your* will be done on earth as it is in heaven." But this is a revolution only God can bring . . . and he will.

This short prayer turns the world upside down. Principalities and powers hear their fall. Dictators are told their time is up. Might will indeed be made right, and truth and justice will prevail. The kingdoms of this world will all pass, giving way to the kingdom of our Lord and of his Christ.

It all comes down to one of the shortest prayers found in the Bible. The Lord's Prayer takes less than twenty seconds to read aloud, but it takes a lifetime to learn. Sadly, most Christians rush through the prayer without learning it—but that is to miss the point completely.

Perhaps this is part of a larger problem. Gary Millar, who has written some enormously helpful resources on prayer, goes so far as to argue that "the evangelical church is slowly but surely giving up on prayer."[1] The statement is shocking, but the truth of his assessment is even more shocking. Why are evangelicals giving up on prayer?

Millar suggests that life is easy for most evangelicals—perhaps too easy. Some of us lack the desperation that most Christians have experienced throughout church history. Desperation leads to prayer. We are also incredibly distracted and busy, states of mind that are enemies of prayer. But giving up on prayer is not only a sign of evangelical weakness. It is also disobedience.

Jesus not only taught his disciples to pray—he also commanded us to pray.

I think there is another big reason behind the fact that so many Christians do not pray. Many Christians simply do not know how to pray.

In the Lord's Prayer, Jesus teaches us how to pray.

We remember Martin Luther as the great Reformer, nailing his famous Ninety-Five Theses to the door of the Castle Church in Wittenberg, Germany, in 1517 and leading the Reformation of the church. What we do not so often remember is that Martin Luther was also a man who regularly needed a haircut. We should be very glad that he did.

Luther's barber, Peter Beskendorf, once asked Luther for advice on how to pray. Luther responded by writing instructions on prayer called "A Simple Way to Pray, for Master Peter the Barber."

Luther pointed his barber to the Lord's Prayer, and he offered this incredibly helpful advice:

> So, as a diligent and good barber, you must keep your thoughts, senses, and eyes precisely on the hair and scissors or razor and not forget where you trimmed or shaved, for, if you want to talk a lot or become distracted thinking about something else, you might well cut someone's nose or mouth or even his throat.[2]

We get Luther's point immediately. We must learn to pray and to resist distractions in prayer. Advice about cutting hair or shaving is easy to understand. A distracted barber is a dangerous barber. Luther applied the lesson well: "How much more does a prayer need to have the undivided attention of the whole heart alone, if it is to be a good prayer!"[3]

We have much to learn about prayer, and the Lord's Prayer is the right place to start. This is no tame prayer for safe times. This is the prayer that turns the world upside down.

So let's learn to pray, taught by Jesus.

CHAPTER 1

THE LORD'S PRAYER

AN OVERVIEW

Several years ago, I was invited to speak at two major conferences back-to-back. The first was on one side of the continent while the second was on the other. Making the coast-to-coast trip in a very limited time was a challenge, and since my talk at the second conference was on a particularly controversial topic, I worked feverishly during my flight to put the finishing touches on my lecture.

The airlines, however, conspired to keep me from landing at my scheduled arrival time, meaning I got only two hours of sleep before I had to deliver my message. Thankfully, I was able to get to the conference and deliver my lecture—after which I promptly sat down in a pew and fell asleep!

The conference, however, was not over. While I slumped in a near-comatose state, one of the hosts approached the podium and said, "We would like to ask Dr. Mohler to come up and pray for us as we conclude." Someone sitting next to me nudged me and politely informed me that I had just been asked to pray.

I blinked, stood up, and made my way to the podium in a fog about what was going on and what I had been asked to do. Thankfully, the host at the podium continued, "Now while Dr. Mohler is coming forward to pray . . . ," providing a welcomed reminder of what was happening.

I found myself at the podium entirely unprepared and knowing nothing about the context of the prayer I'd been asked to deliver. Were we praying for someone specifically? Was someone dying? Were we celebrating something? I did not know. I took a breath, bowed my head, and prayed.

Amazingly, I did what I was asked to do—I led the congregation in prayer. I did so by falling easily into the slipstream of evangelical prayer. I possessed enough familiar prayer language and stock devotional phrases to make it through. While I am certain that many men and women in that congregation prayed sincerely at that moment, I was not one of them. When I finished praying, I did not have the same sense of satisfaction that I had felt at the end of my message. Instead, I had the sense that I had robotically performed a familiar task. It was all too easy—and embarrassing.

My hunch is that many evangelicals can identify with this experience because we know what it is to pray without really praying. Many of us know what it is simply to fall into a pattern of familiar words and slogans without truly engaging our hearts or our minds with the one to whom we speak.

This is similar to the experience I had as a teenager, when I realized after a few months of driving that I could often arrive at a destination and remember almost nothing about the trip there! Driving to some locations, like school, became mindlessly automatic, the entire activity performed by nothing more than instinct. Many evangelicals sense something similar occurring in their prayer life. They can go through the motions, say all the right words, and even lead a congregation or group in prayer without remembering a single word they have said or even understanding what they just prayed for.

These experiences witness to the same reality: prayer is difficult. Like anything of great value, prayer takes great effort, tremendous care, and Spirit-filled discipline. This is one reason why we so desperately need the Lord's Prayer and why we need to sit at the feet of our Lord and implore as the disciples did: "Teach us to pray" (Luke 11:1).

PRAYER IN WORLD RELIGIONS AND IN EVANGELICALISM

Scholars in the field of world religions tell us that prayer, or at least something like prayer, is a part of every major world religion. In Islam, the call of the muezzin summons faithful Muslims to kneel in the direction of Mecca and pray with their heads to the floor. Judaism uses repetitive prayers in formal liturgy and features particular holy sites like the Western Wall in Jerusalem, where worshippers insert scraps of paper with supplications to God into the rock wall. Even Buddhism has a form of prayer that focuses on entering a state of cognitive tranquility—an emptying of the mind of all positive content.

Turning to the different strands of the Christian tradition, we also find a variety of prayer traditions. Roman Catholicism's prayer practices, very much influenced by the monastic tradition and Catholic teachings about Mary, incorporate physical elements like prayer beads and formulaic prayers (e.g., "Hail Mary, full of grace"). Historic Protestantism made prayer into a central theological concern. Martin Luther, John Calvin, and the other magisterial reformers wrote a great deal about prayer, particularly in the context of Christian worship. Their aim was to regulate prayer by Scripture. The Reformers desperately wanted prayer to be understood by the people of God, as opposed to the Latin confession spoken by the priestly caste unfamiliar to most of the congregation. They demanded that prayer be both scriptural and intelligible.

Later, the Anglican Church produced a prayer tradition that is now established in what we know as the *Book of Common Prayer*. These prayers seem exceedingly formal to many modern evangelicals. Yet when Thomas Cranmer first produced this prayer book, solidly based upon Scripture, it was known for its sense of intimacy with God and its use of common language to teach Christians how to pray.

Prayer is also very much a part of our evangelical tradition and our piety. Evangelicals are recognized for a populist approach to prayer. We encourage all saints (that is, all believers) to pray in private and in public.

We regularly organize large prayer meetings and even arrange prayer marathons, which systematize a steady stream of prayer over lengthy periods of time for a single issue. We even teach the youngest among us to pray. But do we teach them well?

PRAYER: THE BAROMETER OF THEOLOGICAL CONVICTION

Pointedly—especially in light of our tendency to pray badly, as noted above—the first thing Jesus taught his disciples about prayer was how *not* to pray. The Lord's Prayer must be seen not only as a model of what prayer *is*, but also as a model of what prayer *is not*. Jesus provided the Lord's Prayer within the context of the Sermon on the Mount (Matt. 5–7), as a corrective to practices that had developed that are familiar to us today, as we shall see.

Prayer is never an isolated event. When we pray, we convey our entire theological system. Our theology is never so clearly displayed before our own eyes and before the world as in our prayers. Praying forces us to articulate our doctrines, convictions, and theological assumptions. These aspects of our Christian life come to a unique focus in prayer because when we speak to God we are explicitly revealing who we believe he is, who we believe we are, what his disposition toward us is, and why he has that disposition.

This point was made by the philosopher Roger Scruton who, even before converting to theism and joining the Church of England, argued that what people truly believe about God is reflected in their worship and prayer: "God is *defined* in the act of worship far more precisely than he is defined by any theology."[1] In other words, what we believe about God is revealed most truly not in what we say about him but in how we approach him—in prayer or in worship. It is one thing to hear a person state what he believes, but it is another thing to listen to him pray. Prayer always reveals the underlying theology. As the old Latin formula reminds us, *Lex orandi, lex credendi*—As we pray, so we believe.

We can safely take Roger Scruton's point one step further: we learn a great deal about someone by what they ask others to pray *for*. Just consider what we learn about the apostle Paul's priorities and character from his prayer requests found all throughout Scripture. For instance, in 2 Thessalonians 3:1–5, Paul's primary prayer was that the gospel advance throughout the world and that the Thessalonians would be deeply impressed with the "love of God" and the "steadfastness of Christ." Clearly, Paul's primary concerns were eternal matters and the kingdom of God.

In short, prayer discloses much about us. It discloses our assumptions and convictions. It discloses our view of God and of ourselves. It discloses our priorities and our assumptions about God's priorities. It discloses our doctrines of God, man, sin, redemption, the world, and a host of other theological matters. If we really want to know what a person believes, we should listen to them pray.

THEOLOGICAL FOUNDATIONS FOR PRAYER

Biblical scholars and pastors from almost every Christian denomination or tradition agree on this much: Christians are called to pray. Yet prayer raises a host of theological issues. What are we trying to do in prayer? Are we trying to convince God to do what he otherwise would not be inclined to do? Are we trying to negotiate with God—even to manipulate him? Are we trying to inform God of what he does not know?

The primary theological foundation for prayer is the fact that there is one true and living God who has revealed himself to us:

> I am the first and I am the last; besides me there is no god. Who is like me? Let him proclaim it. Let him declare and set it before me, since I appointed an ancient people. Let them declare what is to come, and what will happen. Fear not, nor be afraid; have I not told you from of old and declared it? And you are my witnesses! Is there a God besides me? There is no Rock; I know not any. (Isa. 44:6–8)

This God has made us in his image (Gen. 1:26–27), thus we have the spiritual and rational capacity to pray. Part of what it means to be made in the image of God (to bear the *Imago Dei*) is being able to converse with our Creator. We see this in Eden prior to sin entering the world: Adam communed with God (Gen. 2:15–17). Man was made for conversation with God—for communion with the Creator.

Along with affirming what prayer is—communion with God—we should note what prayer is not. First, prayer is not a matter of creative self-expression. In John 4, Jesus, speaking to the woman at the well, said that those who worship the Father must do so "in spirit and truth" (v. 23)—which means we worship God according to who he is and the "truth" he has revealed in his Word. We are not allowed to approach God in any way we see fit. He is holy and exalted, and we know how to come to him only by virtue of his revealed will. Prayer is not an act of spiritual self-expression, nor is any other aspect of worship.

Second, prayer is not an act of therapy. We should not seek some sort of curative kickback when we pray. Some scholars of psychology of religion suggest that people pray because prayer produces serenity and alleviates anxiety and fear. Prayer certainly does often accomplish these things, but prayer also sometimes disrupts our tranquility. God uses prayer to radically reorient our hearts, which can be disturbing. Prayer can sometimes be "anti-therapy." This is because prayer is not first and foremost about us, but about the glory of God.

Third, prayer is not an act of manipulation or persuasion. We are not simply trying to find the right formula or secret code to force God to answer our prayer as we want it to be answered. Nor are we trying to persuade or bargain with God as if he were one of his creations. Prayer is not persuasion. Prayer is about God's will being done—not our own. We must come to God and learn to pray "your will be done" just as Jesus did. If God's will is truly perfect, then why would we want to persuade him to do something that is less than perfect? It is true that Scripture encourages us to bring our deepest concerns, anxieties, and needs before God—the Bible, in fact, is full of illustrations portraying as much—but we must not bring our needs to God thinking that we do so to break down a wall of hostility or complacency. We must bring our needs before God humbly, willing to submit to his perfect plan.

Fourth, prayer is not a news report to the Creator. God knows everything perfectly. This is what Christians mean by saying we worship God as omniscient—he is all-knowing. We must resist the temptation to use prayer as a way of alerting God to what he otherwise does not or would not know. Not only does God know everything—past, present, and future—he even knows our hearts and minds better than we know ourselves. We pray, confident of God's full knowledge but needing to remind ourselves of all our concerns in order to confess our sins, to admit our dependence, to lay out our hearts, and to pray for others. We do not pray to give God our daily briefing, but to bring everything that concerns us before the one who made us.

Finally, prayer is not an act of bargaining. We have all heard prayers that sound like a negotiation meeting: "Lord, I will work on this sin if you will help me with this blessing. Also, I will try to do *this* for you, if you promise to do *that* for me." This type of prayer reveals huge theological misunderstandings. Prayer does not inform God of what he does not know, nor does it get him to do what he is reluctant to do. Prayer does not change God; it changes us. This is not to say that God does not command us to pray or that he does not take our desires in prayer seriously. Rather, we must remember that God is sovereign at all times over all things while simultaneously being loving toward his people. Prayer is not our bargaining chip with a reluctant genie. It is our opportunity to commune with the Creator and Redeemer who loves us.

INTRODUCING THE LORD'S PRAYER

Given our inclination to misunderstand prayer, Scripture regularly reminds us about the true meaning of prayer and how to rightly approach God. Of all the passages in Scripture that speak to prayer, the Lord's Prayer is one of the most astounding and theologically rich. But before we jump into the text, it is important to see how both Matthew and Luke introduce this prayer.

In Luke's account the disciples come to Jesus and ask him, "Lord, teach us to pray, as John taught his disciples" (Luke 11:1). In Matthew's account, the Lord's Prayer stands at the heart of the Sermon on the Mount. Before Jesus gives instructions on praying, he spends a significant amount of time criticizing the prayer practices of the Pharisees, particularly their use of many words and empty phrases. By implication, he may not think much of today's routine Christian prayer either.

The Sermon on the Mount presents a picture of life in the kingdom of heaven. Thus, the contents of the sermon are those issues that Jesus himself identified as essential to that kingdom. The Lord's Prayer is no exception. It stands at the very center of the Sermon on the Mount and so should stand at the very center of our lives as Christ's followers. For this and many other reasons, Christians need to regularly revisit the rich theology of the Lord's Prayer.

The Lord's Prayer in the Sermon on the Mount is part of Christ's vision for life in the inaugurated kingdom of heaven. The arrival of God's kingdom leads to a complete transformation of values that in turn leads to a transformation in piety and practice—particularly in almsgiving, fasting, and prayer.

No one is better able to teach us these transformed values and the nature of true prayer than Jesus himself. The Gospels regularly depict that Jesus engaged in the work of prayer (Matt. 6:5–9; 14:23; 19:13; 26:36–44; Mark 1:35; 6:46; 14:37–39; Luke 3:21; 5:16; 6:12, 28; 9:18, 28–29; 11:1; 22:32, 41, 44; John 17). Perhaps the most prominent example is Jesus' prayer in John 17, typically called Jesus' High Priestly Prayer. Here we get a small glimpse into the richness of Jesus' private prayer life and his intense communion with the Father. Yet prayers like that in John 17 cannot serve as model prayers since many of the elements of Jesus' prayer in John 17 could only be spoken by Christ, the divine-human Mediator. The Lord's Prayer, however, is quite different. The Lord's Prayer is a prayer *for* disciples to pray. Jesus specifically designed it to be used by the people of God and to enrich our prayers. The account of the Lord's Prayer in Matthew makes this point explicitly, for Jesus says, "Pray then like this" (6:9).

But before he gives his model for prayer in Matthew 6, Jesus provides important context:

> And when you pray, you must not be like the hypocrites. For they love to stand and pray in the synagogues and at the street corners, that they may be seen by others. Truly, I say to you, they have received their reward. But when you pray, go into your room and shut the door and pray to your Father who is in secret. And your Father who sees in secret will reward you. And when you pray, do not heap up empty phrases as the Gentiles do, for they think that they will be heard for their many words. Do not be like them, for your Father knows what you need before you ask him. (Matt. 6:5–8)

Matthew 6:1 is the key to understanding this passage. Here Jesus says, "Beware of practicing your righteousness before other people in order to be seen by them, for then you will have no reward from your Father who is in heaven." The first and most urgent warning Jesus gives is a warning against a piety that is public and ostentatious—a piety that is completely vapid and false. This type of piety is self-referential, drawing attention to the one praying, whose actions are designed to reveal him or her to be a pious man or woman.

Jesus shows that something *is* going to be disclosed in our acts of piety—either the glory of God or the superficial, insincere nature of our faith. Jesus is also decidedly clear that those who wish to be seen as pious have already received their reward (v. 5). The Pharisees make themselves look famished and hungry when they fast in order to draw attention to their artificial piety. What they desire are the approving and admiring looks of those who see them. They want to be considered holy by men. They may get what they want—but that is all they will get. Their reward is the praise of man, and that is where their reward ends. Jesus commends another type of piety—a secret piety that will be rewarded by the Father (v. 6). The contrast is stark. We can pursue the glory of the Father by humbling ourselves in secret, or we can pursue our own glory by exalting ourselves before others. We simply cannot do both.

You do not have to be a Pharisee to fall into this trap. Christians sometimes feel the need to impress other believers with their prayers, whether in a worship service or in a smaller group. But authentic prayer is never about impressing anyone. The prayer God seeks is the prayer of the humble and contrite heart. As Jesus said elsewhere, "For everyone who exalts himself will be humbled, but the one who humbles himself will be exalted" (Luke 18:14).

CHAPTER 2

AND WHEN YOU PRAY

WHY JESUS DOESN'T THINK MUCH OF ROUTINE CHRISTIAN PRAYER

MATTHEW 6:5–8

When Jesus begins his instructions to the disciples in Matthew 6 about how to pray, his introductory words— "When you pray"—bear close attention. Note that Jesus does not say, "*If* you pray." He says, "*When* you pray." Jesus expects his disciples to pray. With this opening phrase, he does nothing short of commanding them to do so. A failure to pray is therefore not only a sign of anemic spiritual life, it is disobedience to Christ.

Prayer is central to the Christian life and to the Scriptures. It is interwoven throughout the biblical text, telling us to pray and instructing us how to by showing us the prayers of the Old and New Testament saints and providing us with the Psalter as our guide-book to God-pleasing prayer.

In Scripture it is unthinkable that a true disciple of the Lord Jesus Christ would not pray. Being a disciple of Jesus means following after him, walking as he walked, and doing what he taught. This means praying as he prayed. An active prayer life is assumed.

The four gospels are painstakingly clear that Jesus was a man of prayer. He regularly excused himself from his own disciples to be alone and in intimate communion with the Father (Matt. 14:23; Mark 1:35; Luke 5:16). Moreover, we find Jesus teaching his disciples about the unique power of prayer (Mark 11:24). When they were unable to cast out a demon, Jesus instructed them, "This kind cannot be driven out by anything but prayer" (Mark 9:29).

In short, there is simply no way to reconcile the general prayerlessness of the typical modern American Christian with the teachings of the New Testament and the example of Christ.[1] Moreover, prayer is not simply a Christian's responsibility in obedience to the commands of God and in imitation of the example of Jesus; it is also one of the primary means by which we commune with the living God. There is no true intimacy with God without prayer. The question is *how* we will pray.

BEFORE YOU PRAY: A FEW THINGS JESUS WANTS YOU TO REMEMBER

Do Not Pray Like the Hypocrites

The first thing Jesus tells us as we prepare to pray is "you must not be like the hypocrites" (Matt. 6:5).

Jesus condemned all forms of hypocrisy, but here he is speaking of a specific, public hypocrisy that seeks personal attention for piety, as we have seen. Jesus explains the interior motive of these types of hypocrites: "They love to stand and pray in the synagogues and at the street corners, that they may be seen by others. Truly, I say to you, they have received their reward" (Matt. 6:5).

Jesus is referring here to the ostentatious prayers of the Pharisees, but we need to see the temptation that exists here for us as well. You and I can easily engage in hypocritical prayer that is about God in its formal address but far from him in terms of the posture of our heart.

After instructing his disciples in what not to do, Jesus then tells them what they are supposed to do: "But when you pray, go into your room and shut the door and pray to your Father who is in secret. And your Father who sees in secret will reward you" (v. 6). A private prayer room can be a very useful tool for personal devotion to God, yet Jesus is not concerned primarily with architecture here. He is noting the importance of seclusion. The real issue is not so much where you pray, but doing so in a way that does not parade your piety in front of others.

When we pray in isolation, no temptation exists to pose and posture for any observers. We pray to seek communion with God. The result of praying like this is a reward from the Father in heaven. The Father who knows what is done in secret will reward those who pray in secret. This reward is not material or anything we can quantify. Instead, our reward is communion with God himself. God is the reward he gives to his people.[2]

Do Not Pray to Impress

After admonishing his disciples not to pray to impress people, Jesus then warns them not to pray to impress God: "And when you pray, do not heap up empty phrases as the Gentiles do, for they think that they will be heard for their many words. Do not be like them, for your Father knows what you need before you ask him" (vv. 7–8). God is not looking for long words, long prayers, and mindless repetition. And he is not impressed by the length or complexity of our prayers.

Once, when I was a teenager, I was asked to pray, and I began to repeat words whose meanings I did not know. I had once heard someone use the word *supplication* in prayer, and on this occasion I worked it into my prayer. "Lord," I said, "hear our supplications." After sitting down, I thought, *What in the world is a supplication?* I was then chastened by a thought that remains with me to this day: *What kind of prayer is it that uses words you do not even understand?*

This type of mindless repetition and heaping up of "empty phrases" is powerfully portrayed in 1 Kings 18 at the battle of the gods on Mount Carmel. The priests of Baal were furiously repetitive in their prayers and labored to get the attention of their gods, so much so that they even lacerated their bodies to attract their gods' interest in their activity. Elijah used this as an opportunity to give a little theology of prayer. As the priests continued praying and cutting themselves to no response from Baal, Elijah mocked them by saying, "Cry aloud, for he is a god. Either he is musing, or he is relieving himself, or he is on a journey, or perhaps he is asleep and must be awakened" (v. 27). Then Elijah demonstrated that God is not impressed by our many words.

Elijah's prayer was simple:

> O LORD, God of Abraham, Isaac, and Israel, let it be known this day that you are God in Israel, and that I am your servant, and that I have done all these things at your word. Answer me, O LORD, answer me, that this people may know that you, O LORD, are God, and that you have turned their hearts back. (vv. 36–37)

As this story shows, the Lord isn't looking for impressive words; he is looking for humble hearts— hearts that trust him enough to work, even when our words are few.

Matthew 6:8 is crucial to understanding the Lord's Prayer: "Your Father knows what you need before you ask him." If we understand that our Father knows our needs before we ask him, we won't feel compelled to try to impress God with our prayers and elicit a certain response through some sort of feigned earnestness. Instead, by faith we will see a sovereign God who is ready and able to answer our prayers, and who directs all things for our good and his glory. This type of theology informs how we understand what we are doing when we come before his throne of grace with our requests and needs (Heb. 4:16).

APPROACHING THE LORD'S PRAYER

The Lord's Prayer does not teach us the artifice or the mechanics of prayer. Instead, the Lord Jesus rearranges our theology and breaks open our faulty misconceptions about the character of God and our deepest needs in this world. He teaches us that prayer is not about impressing God; rather, it is about praising him by humbly coming before him to offer the kind of prayer that pleases him.

As Jesus' disciples, we need to pray. We are created to be a praying people. But we desperately need instruction on how to pray. We need the Lord Jesus Christ himself to teach us to pray because, left to our own devices, we will pray wrongly. We need to approach the Lord's Prayer with the same request and attitude as Christ's disciples. We need to ask the Lord to teach us to pray. Of course, Jesus was ready to teach his disciples before they were ready to learn. He is ready to teach us too.

CHAPTER 3

HALLOWING THE FATHER'S NAME

WHERE AUTHENTIC
PRAYER BEGINS

MATTHEW 6:9

The Lord's Prayer reminds us that none other than Jesus himself taught his people to pray—a remarkable truth. The Lord Jesus, because he is fully God and fully man, is the only one truly qualified to teach us how to pray. As the second member of the Trinity, Jesus gives us God's perspective on prayer. In Jesus Christ, God himself is teaching his people how he wants us to approach him. But as one who is fully man, Jesus is also able to instruct us in how we as humans are to approach prayer. Jesus engaged in and experienced a life of prayer. Because he is fully human without any taint of sin, Jesus led a life of perfect prayer. Jesus knows what it is to pray because he shares our nature and even now is interceding for us at the right hand of God (Heb. 7:25). We must never forget, then, the tremendous opportunity we have when we read the Lord's Prayer. In Matthew 6, Jesus teaches his disciples to pray—words from God himself about the prayer that he desires.

As mentioned in chapter 1, our prayers reveal our deepest convictions about God, about ourselves, and about the world around us. Every word we utter in prayer, every idea and concept that we form as we pray, and every emotion that flows out of our heart is a reflection of what we believe about God and about the gospel of Christ. The well-known Christian formula "As we believe, so we pray" underlies this very reality. Nothing uncovers the true state of our souls, both to ourselves and to others, as does prayer.

As we approach Jesus' teachings on prayer, we should ask ourselves: How do Jesus' words correct any bad prayer habits I have developed? How is Jesus challenging my prayer life and inviting me to enter into a more God-glorifying pattern of prayer?

As the Old Testament makes clear over and over again, God does not take the worship of himself lightly (see for instance Lev. 10:1–2). God regulates and sets the parameters for our worship, not us. Just consider the scrupulous detail God gave to Moses about how the tabernacle was to be constructed and how the priests were to conduct themselves during sacrifice and worship. The implication was clear: God was warning Israel not to lean on her own creativity when it came to approaching the Lord God in worship.

This raises one of the most fundamental issues about prayer: Where do we start? Every prayer has to begin somewhere. How do we enter the heavenly court and speak to almighty God? Beginning in Matthew 6:9, Jesus provides us with an answer, saying, "Pray then like this."

THERE IS NO "I" IN PRAYER: COMBATING INDIVIDUALISM IN OUR PRAYERS

Over the past several decades I have noticed that many Christians tend to begin their prayers by presenting their needs. Of course, in some sense, I understand why we naturally turn to petition almost immediately upon entering into prayer. After all, prayer reminds us of our deep need for God to sanctify us in our circumstances and save us from our trials. Additionally, our circumstances and trials are often the very things that drive us to pray in the first place. Thus the tyranny of the urgent has a remarkable way of consuming our intellectual life and our thought patterns. As a result, our prayers, from beginning to end, are often marked by petition.

But the Lord's Prayer begins in a very different place. Petitions certainly are a part (a major part, in fact) of the Lord's Prayer, but Jesus does not begin with requests. He begins, instead, by identifying the character of the God to whom he prays while at the same time challenging our individualism in prayer. Jesus does all this in the first two words, "Our Father."

The word *our*, at first glance, seems like an insignificant little pronoun. But Jesus is making a tremendously powerful theological point by beginning his prayer with the word *our*. Jesus is reminding us that when we enter into a relationship with God, we enter into a relationship with his people. When we are saved *by* Christ, we are saved *into* his body, the church. In fact, this emphasis on our place in the corporate identity of the church is reiterated throughout the prayer. One way to notice this emphasis is simply to read through the prayer and stress each first-person personal pronoun: "*Our* Father in heaven, hallowed be your name. Your kingdom come, your will be done, on earth as it is in heaven. Give *us* this day *our* daily bread, and forgive *us our* debts, as *we* also have forgiven *our* debtors. And lead *us* not into temptation, but deliver *us* from evil."

Do you notice what is stunningly absent? There is no first-person singular pronoun in the entire prayer! Jesus did not teach us to pray, "*My* Father who is heaven. . . . Give *me* this day *my* daily bread and forgive *me my* debts as *I* also have forgiven *my* debtors. And lead *me* not into temptation but deliver *me* from evil." The point is not to deny our own sins or our own needs, but to never leave the focus solely on ourselves.

One of the besetting sins of evangelicalism is our obsession with individualism. The first-person singular pronoun reigns in our thinking. We tend to think about nearly everything (including the truths of God's Word) only as they relate to *me*. Yet when Jesus teaches his disciples to pray, he emphasizes from the very outset that we are part of a corporate people called the church. God is not merely "my Father." He is "our Father"— the Father of my brothers and sisters in the faith with whom I identify and with whom I pray.

If we are honest, even many of our prayer meetings fail to take into account Jesus' emphasis on the corporate character of prayer. Yet we must never lose sight of the fact that even when we pray by ourselves (Matt. 6:6), we must pray with an eye toward and with love for Christ's church. We must remember the pattern of our Lord's speech in the model prayer and recall not only the words he used but the words he didn't use. The first-person singular (*I*, *me*, *my*, *mine*) is completely absent from the Lord's Prayer. Evidently, prayer should not center on you or me.

The problem of overemphasizing ourselves in our prayers reminds me of G. K. Chesterton's famous answer to a question put forth by a major newspaper, "What is the problem with the world?" This question was sent to many public intellectuals in Victorian England, many of whom sent back long essays delineating the complexities of everything wrong with the world. Reputedly, Chesterton responded with a simple handwritten note that read, "I am. Sincerely yours, Chesterton."

What is the biggest problem with our prayers? Perhaps the most fundamental answer mirrors Chesterton's: "I am." One of our greatest problems and deficiencies in prayer is that we begin with our own concerns and our own petitions without regard for our brothers and sisters. Many of us falter in prayer because we begin with the wrong word: *I* instead of *our*. Jesus reminds us that we are part of a family, even when we pray. Thus the first word of Jesus' model prayer is the word *our*. We are in this together.

To be a Christian is to be a part of the church of the

Lord Jesus Christ. By God's grace we are incorporated into the body of Christ so that our most fundamental spiritual identity is not an "I" but a "we." This runs against the grain of our fallen state. This also runs against the grain of American individualism—an individualism that has seeped into many sections of evangelicalism. But we must be normed by Scripture. Jesus teaches us to drop the "I" and start with "our."

A FATHER IN HEAVEN: OUR IMMINENT AND TRANSCENDENT GOD

A Father

God is identified by many titles throughout Scripture. He is called "Lord," "Most High," "Almighty," "King," even "the judge of all the earth." Yet in the Lord's Prayer, Jesus does not refer to God by any of these titles. Instead, he refers to him as "Father." By using this word, Jesus reminds us that God is not some anonymous deity or impersonal force. We pray to the God of Scripture, the one who has revealed himself in the Old and New Testaments. Yet we come to this God by the work of Christ, and we have a unique relationship with him. As our Father, the one who hears our prayers is imminent—that is intimately near—to his people.

The term *Father* is not merely a title for God. In fact, we must use great care in how we define the "fatherhood of God." Jesus is here affirming a filial relationship that exists between the Creator and those who have been saved through faith in Jesus Christ and adopted into God's family. But beginning in the late nineteenth and early twentieth centuries, the term "fatherhood of God" has often been used to imply that God is a father to all people, without distinction and without regard for a person's faith in Christ.

Of course, there is a sense in which God is fatherly toward all his creation. But Scripture affirms that we only come to know God as our Father *personally* when through faith in Christ we are adopted into God's family. The 2000 Baptist Faith and Message, the Southern Baptist Convention's statement of faith, summarizes this quite well:

> God as Father reigns with providential care over His universe, His creatures, and the flow of the stream of human history according to the purposes of His grace. He is all powerful, all knowing, all loving, and all wise. God is Father in truth to those who become children of God through faith in Jesus Christ. He is fatherly in His attitude toward all men.[1]

Indeed, God is fatherly toward all his creation. God exercises a "providential care" over the works of his hands. He is fatherly in relationship to everything he has made and everyone he has made. The fact that any human being anywhere exists and lives and breathes is a testimony to a paternal and benevolent relationship between the Creator and his creation. But as the confession of faith points out, God is *properly* Father only to those who know him through the Son.

Scripture attests to the unique fatherly relationship God has with his people on numerous occasions:

> In love he predestined us for adoption to himself as sons through Jesus Christ, according to the purpose of his will. (Eph. 1:4–5)

> But when the fullness of time had come, God sent forth his Son, born of woman, born under the law, to redeem those who were under the law, so that we might receive adoption as sons. (Gal. 4:4–5)

> For all who are led by the Spirit of God are sons of God. For you did not receive the spirit of slavery to fall back into fear, but you have received the Spirit of adoption as sons, by whom we cry, "Abba! Father!" The Spirit himself bears witness with our spirit that we are children of God, and if children, then heirs—heirs of God and fellow heirs with Christ, provided we suffer with him in order that we may also be glorified with him. (Rom. 8:14–17)

These passages make very clear that our sonship and our ability to relate to God as Father come only through redemption. Ephesians 1:5 indicates that we are predestined to adoption "through Jesus Christ"— that is, according to and on the basis of Christ's work on the cross. Galatians 4:4–5 emphasizes this same point by showing that our redemption from the law results in sonship. Finally, Paul made clear in Romans 8:14–17, only those who have the Spirit of God (called the "Spirit of adoption") can call out to God as "Abba! Father!"

Scripture is thus unambiguous. We can only relate to God as Father because we have received the Spirit of adoption as sons and daughters through the objective, atoning work of Jesus Christ. In other words, we can call God "Father" not because we are his children by virtue of being his creation, but because we are his children by virtue of adoption. Our Father has adopted us through his Son, in his Son, to his own glory.

We see, then, that Jesus teaches us to begin our prayers according to gospel realities. When we pray, we are praying from within the context of an established relationship that Christ himself has enacted, effected, and achieved. Only by virtue of Jesus' work on the cross can we truly say, "Our Father in heaven."

These truths also remind us that we do not approach God's throne in prayer because we have the right in and of ourselves to do so. Our ability to come into God's presence ended in Genesis 3. Only by God's grace and mercy through the atoning work of Christ do we now have the right to stand before the God of all creation and speak the words "Our Father in heaven."

The theologian Gary Millar has observed that the Lord's Prayer is necessary precisely because the unbroken communion Adam and Eve experienced with God in the garden of Eden ended with their sin and expulsion from the garden.[2] Adam conversed with God in the garden in the cool of the day. We are no longer in the garden of Eden. However, because we have been adopted as sons and daughters of God, those who are in Christ can truly pray to God as "our Father."

Furthermore, the word *Father* also says something about God's disposition toward us. Whereas we were once God's enemies, now, in Christ, God loves us no less than he loves his own Son. This gospel relationship tells us that God, our Father, is pleased and even glad to receive the prayers of his children. Thus, in these two small introductory words, Jesus reminds us of the gospel and the gracious disposition God has toward us. The God who has delivered us from our sins is also the Father who loves us and welcomes us. The God who saved us by the work of Christ on the cross is the same God who invites us to become part of his family. The God who so graciously spoke to us in and through his Son now remarkably invites us to come speak to him. He is both transcendent and imminent—in Christ he is close to us.

A Father in Heaven

Jesus' address emphasizes not only God's immanence in calling him Father but also his transcendence by referring to him as the "Father *in heaven*." God is not merely a benevolent force in the universe or some tribal deity. This is the God who rules and reigns from on high. This is the God enthroned over all creation who enjoys the unending worship of the angelic host. This is our high and holy God. Our Father is in heaven; he is transcendent.

This mention of God's transcendence is a reminder that God is distinct from his creation. Even though we have a precious relationship with God made possible by the work of Christ, we should not therefore think that God is simply a grandfatherly figure in the sky or worse, "the man upstairs." Jesus shows us that even as we can come to God as his children and approach a loving Father, we must not forget that the Father to whom we come is none other than the almighty God of the universe.

The transcendence of God is emphasized time and again throughout the Old Testament.

> Know therefore today, and lay it to your heart, that the LORD is God in heaven above and on the earth beneath; there is no other. (Deut. 4:39)

> There is none like God, O Jeshurun, who rides through the heavens to your help, through the skies in his majesty. (Deut. 33:26)

> For you, O LORD, are most high over all the earth; you are exalted far above all gods. (Ps. 97:9)

In Ecclesiastes 5:2, Solomon connected our understanding of the transcendence of God to the proper practice of prayer. He wrote, "Be not rash with your mouth, nor let your heart be hasty to utter a word before God, for God is in heaven and you are on earth. Therefore let your words be few." Our knowledge of God's transcendence should shape our prayers by reminding us that prayer is a humble and reverent enterprise. This is why I believe that one of the most helpful things to do in prayer is to pray the Scriptures. In this way, we can make sure that God's words are many and that our words are comparatively few.

THE GRACE OF DIVINE DISCLOSURE

Before leaving the words "Our Father in heaven," we should note one last important feature of this passage: we do not name God; he names himself. This may seem like an odd observation, but it has enormous theological implications. When Jesus appropriates Old Testament language to address God instead of opting for newer, more "creative" ways to address him, he is reminding us that we must only speak about God as he has revealed himself.

Moses' encounter with God at the burning bush makes this point abundantly clear. God commissioned Moses to speak to Pharaoh and demand that he let the Israelites go. Moses understood the importance of knowing the name of the God who sent him and thus asked, "Whom shall I say has sent me? What is your name?" (Ex. 3:13, author's paraphrase). The book of Exodus does not shy away from portraying the full breadth of Moses' imperfections. Yet one thing Moses does understand is that he has no right to name God. Only God has that right. As Carl Henry stated, when God reveals himself he is forfeiting "his own personal privacy that his creatures might know him."[3] Therefore, we must take note of what God says about himself and speak about him and to him according to those truths.

When we pray, therefore, we must follow Jesus' model of only ascribing attributes and names to God that God himself has employed. We are not free to call him what we want. This point is particularly important in our day since feminist theologians and others promoting inclusive language proposals have posited that gender-specific designations for God are archaic and patriarchal. In light of this, many theologians have asserted that we should use feminine attributions for God as well as masculine, such as "heavenly Mother." Others have asserted that because human fathers often so poorly exercise their parental responsibilities and abusively employ their authority, the very language of fatherhood may turn people away from God.

How should evangelicals who affirm the inerrancy of Scripture respond? First, we must recognize that Scripture is very clear that God is neither male nor female. Instead God is spirit (John 4:24); he has no biological features. Second, we must also assert that according to Scripture God is rightly understood as a Father to his children. Theologians often categorize this type of language in Scripture as "analogical" language. In other words, God's descriptions of himself to us are accommodated for our creaturely understanding. This does not mean that these descriptions are in any way untrue or false. Rather, God speaks in a way that communicates reality but in a way our minds can understand. Thus, altering God's self-designation in any way changes his intended analogy and thus destroys the truth of his Word.

Ultimately, God has not revealed himself as a heavenly mother. God prescribes the vocabulary we ought to use when addressing him. If we wish to honor our transcendent Father, we will follow the example of Jesus and speak in accord with what God has revealed of himself in Scripture. When we pray "our Father," we are rejecting every misrepresentation of God's character, every lie of the Devil, every heresy of idolatry, and praying to the one, true, and loving God—our Father.

HALLOWED BE THY NAME: JESUS' FIRST REQUEST

After Jesus identifies the character of God, showing us how we are to address him, he moves to the first petition, "hallowed be your name." Many Christians mistakenly believe that this phrase is yet another exclamation of praise. But this phrase is actually an appeal. Jesus is not merely saying that God's name *is* hallowed; rather, he is asking God to make his name hallowed. In order to understand this petition, we must first consider the meaning of two crucial words: *hallowed* and *name*.

First, what does the word *hallowed* mean? *Hallow* and *hallowed* are archaic words that have largely dropped out of our modern vocabulary and have not been replaced by anything else (a fact that reveals something about the secularization of our culture). For many, the word *hallow* may even seem a bit ghoulish since the only time modern Americans use this word is with regard to Halloween. The verb *hallow*, however, simply means to "make holy" or "consider as holy." Thus, when Jesus petitions God to hallow his name, he is asking that God act in such a way that he visibly demonstrates his holiness and his glory. We will explore just how this happens later.

Second, what does it mean for God to hallow his *name*? The first thing to recognize about this request is that God's "name" is essentially shorthand for God himself. The Old Testament regularly refers to God simply by referring to God's "name." But it is also the case that God's name often refers to his public reputation. Just as we speak of "having a good name" as a way to refer to a good reputation, the Old Testament uses the same idiom to refer to God's reputation. Herman Bavinck, the prolific nineteenth-century Dutch theologian, beautifully explained this point in his *Reformed Dogmatics*:

> All we can learn about God from his revelation is designated his Name in Scripture. . . . A name is something personal and very different from a number or a member of a species. It always feels more or less unpleasant when others misspell or garble our name: it stands for our honor, our worth, our person, and individuality. . . . There is an intimate link between God and his name. According to Scripture, this link is not accidental or arbitrary but forged by God himself. We do not name God; he names himself. . . . Summed up in his name, therefore, is his honor, his fame, his excellencies, his entire revelation, his very being.[4]

This explains why God is so concerned with his
name throughout Scripture. For instance, God repeatedly indicates that when he acts he does so for the sake
of his name, that is for his own glory.

> *For your name's sake*, O LORD, pardon my guilt,
> for it is great. (Ps. 25:11)

> Bring my sons from afar and my daughters from
> the end of the earth, everyone who is called by my
> name, *whom I created for my glory.* (Isa. 43:6–7)

> *For my name's sake* I defer my anger; *for the sake
> of my praise* I restrain it for you, that I may not
> cut you off. Behold, I have refined you, but not
> as silver; I have tried you in the furnace of afflic-
> tion. *For my own sake, for my own sake*, I do it, for
> *how should my name be profaned? My glory I will
> not give to another.* (Isa. 48:9–11)

> *I acted for the sake of my name, that it should not
> be profaned* in the sight of the nations, in whose
> sight I had brought them out. (Ezek. 20:14)

> Therefore say to the house of Israel, Thus says
> the Lord GOD: It is not for your sake, O house of
> Israel, that I am about to act, but *for the sake of
> my holy name.* (Ezek. 36:22)

The petition "hallowed be your name" is essentially
a summary of these Old Testament passages. By asking

that the name of God be "hallowed," Jesus is asking God
to so move and act in the world that people value his
glory, esteem his holiness, and treasure his character
above all else. We must not miss this: Jesus' first request
is not that his personal needs be met, but that God's
glory and holiness be known and loved as it deserves.
What a remarkably God-centered prayer.

How then does God "hallow his name" in the
world? First, "hallowed be your name" is a request that
the church be sanctified. The church is the steward
of God's name. One of the most important ecclesial
responsibilities is to bear the name of God faithfully. Every single Christian who comes to know the
Lord Jesus Christ as Savior and is adopted as a son
or daughter of God bears this responsibility. This is
a remarkable task—a task for which we are not sufficient. This is, of course, why we must pray this request
like Jesus. We must petition God to "hallow his name"
in our discipleship, in our prayer, in our preaching,
in our witnessing, in our work, and in eternity. Our
ultimate concern is not that our lives be comfortable,
but that God be glorified, and that our lives, even our
prayers, put God's glory on display.

Of course, God's inherent glory does not wax and
wane. We cannot add to or take away anything from
God's inherent majesty. But his visible and observable
glory can be made more or less apparent depending
on our faithfulness. Faithfulness in the Christian life
makes the glory of God go public. The church must
therefore remember that the degree to which God's
glory is manifested on earth depends on how we

conduct ourselves as his redeemed image bearers. Even in our prayer we are to begin in the right place by understanding that our central aim is to be a holy people set apart unto the one who has created, saved, and redeemed us. In this way, when the world looks to those who are in Christ, the holiness of God is amplified and made invariably visible.

Second, "hallowed be your name" is also an evangelistic petition. This opening line of the Lord's Prayer is a clear reminder to us that when any sinner comes to faith in the Lord Jesus Christ and his or her sins are forgiven, God's holy name is shown to be evermore holy in the eyes of the church and of the world. And the more people there are who come to know Christ, the more people exist who revere God's character and hallow his name. Thus, God's saving of a sinner shows God's glory and, in turn, the saved sinner proclaims to the world the excellencies of the God who saved him. God's name is thus hallowed in the world.

The first line of Jesus' prayer focuses our attention on God and not on ourselves. Jesus teaches us that God is our imminent Father. He is the transcendent one *in heaven*. He is the one who reveals and names himself. And our chief concern in prayer is not our own comfort but God's glory. If we do not truly know the God to whom we speak, our prayers will remain impotent, facile, and devoid of life. Only by coming to know the God that Jesus describes in the first line of the Lord's Prayer will we be moved to come before the throne of grace. As J. I. Packer noted:

Men who know their God are before anything else men who pray, and the first point where their zeal and energy for God's glory come to expression is in their prayers . . . If there is little energy for such prayer, and little consequent practice of it, this is a sure sign that as yet we scarcely know our God.[5]

Indeed, a paltry understanding of God leads to paltry prayers. If we come to know and love the God and Father of our Lord Jesus Christ, we will be motivated to pray and to pray as Jesus taught us.

CHAPTER 4

YOUR KINGDOM COME

WHOSE AGENDA IS OUR CONCERN ANYWAY?

MATTHEW 6:10

The first petition in the Lord's Prayer is that God's name be hallowed. The second petition, "your kingdom come," builds on the first by showing us how God's name is hallowed in the world. God reveals his character and reputation as his kingdom spreads to every corner of the earth and as citizens of that kingdom do God's will on earth as it is in heaven. But what is God's kingdom, and what does it mean to pray for its arrival?

A RADICAL AND REVOLUTIONARY PRAYER

Very few prayers become cemented in the public consciousness. The Lord's Prayer is of course one, but others, considerably more trite, have also become cultural artifacts. For instance, the so-called Serenity Prayer: "God grant me the serenity to accept the things I cannot change, courage to change the things I can, and wisdom to know the difference." A great deal of controversy surrounds who first wrote the Serenity Prayer, though the most likely candidate seems to be theologian Reinhold Niebuhr.

The Serenity Prayer has enjoyed the spotlight since it was first penned. It has been adopted, for instance, by groups such as Alcoholics Anonymous and other humanitarian or self-help organizations. It has been placarded and painted on decorative pieces throughout the country. The comic strip *Calvin and Hobbes* even spoofed the prayer, perhaps writing a superior version in the process, by depicting the young child Calvin praying, "Lord grant me the strength to change what I can, the inability to accept what I can't, and the incapacity to know the difference."

In many ways the Serenity Prayer is the model prayer for a post-Christian society. It says nothing about the character of God, the plight of man, the need for redemption, or the nature of the gospel. The Serenity Prayer is nothing more than a generic prayer for a people with generic religious convictions.

The Lord's Prayer, however, is doctrinally robust, theologically deep, and anything but serene. The Lord's Prayer is anything but tame. Regrettably, our familiarity often blinds us from seeing just how radical, even subversive, this prayer is. It is for those who hold firmly that Jesus Christ has inaugurated a kingdom, has risen from the dead, reigns at the right hand of God, and is coming again to judge the living and the dead. The Lord's Prayer is for revolutionaries, for men and women who want to see the kingdoms of this world give way to the kingdom of our Lord.

WHAT IS THE KINGDOM OF GOD? LEARNING FROM THE THEOLOGICAL TRADITION

Augustine's City of God

When Jesus prays "your kingdom come," what exactly is he asking of the Father? What is the kingdom of God? That question is one of the oldest and most hotly contested theological issues in the Christian church. Augustine, the bishop of Hippo in the fifth century, addressed it at length in his magisterial *The City of God*, written after the fall of the Roman Empire. In the post-Reformation period, the Lutheran tradition developed what is known as "Two Kingdom Theology," parsing out the distinctions between what properly belongs to man's kingdom and what properly belongs to God's kingdom. Later, in the nineteenth century, classic dispensationalism taught that the kingdom was a purely future reality, inaugurated at the millennial reign of Christ.

Among these attempts at explaining the kingdom of God, Augustine's *City of God* has proven the most helpful and the most in line with the teachings of Scripture. This work was birthed out of Augustine's reflections

on the demise of the so-called eternal city—the city of
Rome. More pointedly, Augustine was trying to answer
the question: "To what degree should the church care
about the fall of Rome or does this ultimately teach us
that politics do not matter? Is this in any way related
to the church's gospel witness?" Augustine's answer
to these questions was profoundly *eschatological*—
looking to the final consummation of God's plan.

Augustine employed the metaphor of a city, a *polis*,
to describe the kingdom of God and the kingdoms of
this world. Building upon Jesus' teaching about the
first and the second greatest commandments (Matt.
22:36–40), Augustine suggested that the Christian
must understand that there are two cities in the world.
The first city is the City of God. This city is God's not
merely because he resides there but because his character and authority define it. There, God's sovereign
authority is unmitigated and unconditioned. It is
ordered according to the rule and reign of God's law,
which demonstrates simultaneously and in equal pro-
portion his justice, righteousness, mercy, and holiness.
Thus in the City of God, everything is exactly as God
would have it to be. The longing of every Christian is
to live in that city.

By God's grace and the power of the gospel, Paul
indicated that we have already been made citizens of
the City of God (Phil. 3:20). This citizenship is given
to us by divine promise, though we do not yet reside
there. Until we do, every Christian lives in and experiences quite a different city—the City of Man. Jesus
Christ is Lord and ultimately sovereign, yet he is also

patient and allows human beings to exercise moral responsibility.

As a result, the City of Man is not as it should be. Unlike the City of God, the City of Man is characterized by selfishness, ungodliness, conflict, and strife. The City of Man is temporary—both conditioned and created. It does not exist on its own terms, though as Paul made clear in Romans 1 the City of Man refuses to acknowledge its creaturely and dependent status. Augustine thought it crucial to understand that the City of God is a coming thing never to pass away, while the City of Man is even now a passing thing. And he warned the church not to confuse the one for the other. The warning remains for the church today.

Augustine also argued that both cities are characterized by a primary love. The love of man animates the City of Man, even as the love of God animates the City of God. The problem with the love that animates the City of Man is that it is self-absorbed and full of selfish ambition. In other words, on this side of Genesis 3 we only love those of our own tribe, clan, or family. The love that animates the City of Man is not expansive and selfless. Instead, it fiercely guards our own interests.

With Rome as the model of the City of Man, Augustine's words proved true before the church's very eyes. Augustine's work revealed to the church that even while Rome was at its height, it was already crumbling because it was built on the wrong love. In contrast, even though the church may seem weak, ineffective, and inglorious, it alone will endure because it is built on true love of God and the things of God. If we fail to see this, we do so because we tend to see the *passing thing* as a *coming thing* and the *coming thing* as a *passing thing*.

Augustine's discussion of the two cities reminds us that the kingdom of God is not something that is part of the political systems of this world. No government on earth truly represents God's kingdom. Instead, Christians are citizens of a kingdom that will one day arrive in consummate glory. Our hope is not that the governments of this world will transform into the kingdom of God, but that the kingdom of God will come from heaven to earth in power and glory.

Recent Evangelical Scholarship and a Biblical Theology of the Kingdom

In the twentieth century a number of faithful evangelical scholars such as George Eldon Ladd reinvigorated our understanding of the kingdom.[1] They demonstrated that in Scripture the kingdom of God must be understood as something that is already here on earth but not yet *fully* present. In other words, the kingdom of God has been *inaugurated* but not yet *consummated*. As Ladd and others pointed out, the kingdom of God is essentially the end-of-history, or eschatological, vision of the Old Testament. The authors of the Old Testament envisioned a day when God would send the Messiah to triumph over Israel's enemies, establish the throne of David, and reign in righteousness.

This kingdom arrived with the coming of Christ,

who urged his hearers to repent because the "kingdom of God is at hand." Christians are now part of that kingdom. As Paul stated, "[God] has delivered us from the domain of darkness and transferred us to the kingdom of his beloved Son" (Col. 1:13). Thus, even though we await the full expression of God's kingdom that will come in glory and power at the return of Christ, we are at this time living under the reign of God as his people—we are citizens of that kingdom.

Even so, the question remains, "What is the kingdom of God?" The answer is found in the way the Bible speaks about God's kingdom in terms of creation, the fall, redemption, and consummation.

Graeme Goldsworthy has defined the kingdom of God as "God's people in God's place under God's rule and blessing."² Each of these features is present in the earliest manifestation of God's kingdom in the garden of Eden. God's people, Adam and Eve, live in God's place, the garden of Eden, under God's rule and blessing. The fall completely disrupts the kingdom. Adam and Eve are exiled from the garden, no longer able to enjoy God's blessing because they rebelled against God's rule. Indeed, apart from redemption, rebellion is the state of every natural man. We are all born east of Eden, traitors to the crown, and living in what Paul calls the "kingdom of darkness" (Col. 1:13).

But God did not leave this world in darkness. In the work of redemption, God continued the work of building a kingdom on earth. Thus, God called Abraham and his children (God's people) to be a light to the nations (Isa. 42:6; 49:6). He promised them the land of Canaan (God's place) where he would dwell with them in the tabernacle and then in the temple. Finally, God gave the Israelites his law and the sacrificial system so that they might draw near to him (God's rule and blessing). Yet, as we all know, Israel failed to do and to be what God desired of them. Like Adam, they rebelled against God. Even their kings, those who were supposed to represent the nation, were almost to a man rebellious and wicked, often leading the people to worship false gods.

As a result, God sent Israel into exile in Babylon, just as he expelled Adam from the garden. Yet even in the midst of this judgment, the prophets spoke of a day when God would fully and finally bring his kingdom from heaven to earth. Jeremiah, for instance, spoke of a day when God would inaugurate a new covenant, when the law would no longer be written on tablets of stone but would instead be written on the tablets of people's hearts. In other words, the law would no longer only be something outside of us (demanding obedience and condemning our failure) but instead would be something God etched on our hearts, giving us the power to obey his commands.

Perhaps nowhere in the Old Testament is this hope for the inauguration of God's kingdom painted more vividly than in the Davidic covenant in 2 Samuel 7:8–17:

> Now, therefore, thus you shall say to my servant David, "Thus says the Lord of hosts, I took you from the pasture, from following the sheep, that you should

be prince over my people Israel. And I have been with you wherever you went and have cut off all your enemies before you. And I will make for you a great name, like the name of the great ones of the earth. And I will appoint a place for my people Israel and will plant them, so that they may dwell in their own place and be disturbed no more. And violent men shall afflict them no more, as formerly, from the time that I appointed judges over my people Israel. And I will give you rest from all your enemies. Moreover, the Lord declares to you that the Lord will make you a house. When your days are fulfilled and you lie down with your fathers, I will raise up your offspring after you, who shall come from your body, and I will establish his kingdom. He shall build a house for my name, and I will establish the throne of his kingdom forever. I will be to him a father, and he shall be to me a son. When he commits iniquity, I will discipline him with the rod of men, with the stripes of the sons of men, but my steadfast love will not depart from him, as I took it from Saul, whom I put away from before you. And your house and your kingdom shall be made sure forever before me. Your throne shall be established forever." In accordance with all these words, and in accordance with all this vision, Nathan spoke to David.

This passage points to the coming kingdom ("the house") that God will build. God promised that a descendent of David will have a kingdom established "forever." While Solomon is the immediate son in view in this passage (the one who receives correction when he commits iniquity), the ultimate fulfillment of this text is none other than Jesus Christ. As Acts 2 makes abundantly clear, Jesus sits on the throne of David, reigning over the universe. His kingdom is unchallenged and his reign is without end.

As already noted, Jesus came preaching the inauguration of the kingdom. His disciples were allowed a glimpse of his kingdom in glory during the transfiguration (Matt. 17:2; Mark 9:2). Jesus' work on the cross is the work of a king who has come to rescue his people. And after his resurrection Jesus declared that he had been given "all authority in heaven and on earth" (Matt. 28:18). The Great Commission is rooted in Christ's declaration that he is the king on the throne of all creation. In our current stage in redemptive history, therefore, God's kingdom is made up of those who believe in Christ (God's people) gathered in local churches across the world (God's place) under the law of Christ and partaking of the new covenant (God's rule and blessing).

Of course, we still wait for the day when this kingdom will be consummated. As of right now, the people of God are at war with spiritual darkness. We are carrying out a commission to make disciples of the king and citizens of the kingdom. And, of course, we can only do so with great suffering and tribulation. Thus, while we are indeed in God's kingdom, we still await God's kingdom in its fullness. We still await the completion of the Great Commission. We still await the coming of the king and the destruction of all wickedness. We long for the day when we will no longer be the church militant, but the church triumphant. Revelation 11:15 describes just what that day of consummation will bring: "Then the seventh angel blew his trumpet, and there were loud voices in heaven, saying, 'The kingdom of the world has become the kingdom of our Lord and of his Christ, and he shall reign forever and ever.'"

Now we have a few key insights helpful in interpreting this petition—"your kingdom come"—in the Lord's Prayer. God's kingdom is essentially his reign over his people for their good and his glory. God's reign is not just his absolute sovereignty; it is also a redemptive reign that transforms hearts and creates obedience.

THE COMING KINGDOM

This leads to a further question: According to Scripture, how does the kingdom of God come from heaven to earth? Many horribly wrong answers to that question have been given in history. Theological liberals in the early twentieth century argued that the kingdom of God arrived through moral reform and social justice. This view, sometimes called the "social gospel" and championed by theologians like Walter Rauschenbusch, saw the kingdom of God as something humanity itself could achieve through social action.

Theological conservatives have sometimes also erred in thinking that Christians can usher in the kingdom through political action and cultural influence. The problem with this way of thinking is, of course, that Jesus' kingdom is not of this world (John 18:36). Political power and cultural influence are not unimportant, but they can never change the hearts of sinners nor provide the forgiveness of sins.

The Bible teaches that God's kingdom only comes as God's people preach God's Word, which, coupled with God's Spirit, produces life and obedience. To use the language of Paul, God's Word and Spirit change the hearts of sinners such that they are rescued out of the kingdom of darkness and into the kingdom of his dear Son (Col. 1:13). As Phil Ryken put it, "The kingdom comes mainly through proclamation, through the announcement that Christ, who was crucified, is now King. . . . The only way people ever come into God's kingdom is by hearing his heralds proclaim a crucified king."[3]

THE REIGN AND RULE OF GOD: YOUR WILL BE DONE

Having instructed the disciples to ask for God's kingdom to come, Jesus then tells them to pray, "Your will be done." Scripture does not use the term "will of God" uniformly. Rather, as theologians have recognized for centuries, the "will of God" can be used in two different ways. First, Scripture can speak of God's will of decree, or what we could call God's sovereign will. When Scripture speaks of God's will in this sense, it refers to his absolute, sovereign rule over all things. The only reason anything exists is because God has willed it to exist. Indeed, from the movement of the smallest particles of sand to the political actions of world powers, every event in the cosmos is ordered and orchestrated by the will of God. The apostle Paul spoke of God's will in this sense in Ephesians 1:11, when he affirmed that God works "all things according to the counsel of his will." Everything that God has willed shall infallibly come to pass.

Scripture speaks of God's sovereign will on almost every page. In Genesis 1, God created simply by speaking and willing the cosmos into existence. God showed his sovereignty over the kingdoms of the earth and even hardened Pharaoh's heart in order to show his glory in rescuing Israel in the exodus (Ex. 9:12; 10:20, 27; cf. Rom. 9:17–18). God himself proclaimed his superiority over all the false gods of the nations by declaring the absolute rule of his will over creation. In Isaiah, God said that he alone declared "the end from the beginning" and proclaimed, "My counsel shall stand, and I will accomplish all my purpose" (46:10). In sum, as the psalmist exclaimed, "Our God is in the heavens; he does all that he pleases" (Ps. 115:3).

Second, Scripture uses the phrase "will of God" to refer to God's commandments. Theologians also refer to this use of the "will of God" as God's *revealed* will. The revealed will of God speaks to what God expects of his human creatures. The Ten Commandments, for instance, are an excellent example of God's revealed will. The call to repent and believe the gospel would be yet another example of God's revealed will (Acts 17:30). Paul very clearly referred to God's revealed will in 1 Thessalonians 4:3 when he wrote, "This is the will of God, your sanctification: that you abstain from sexual immorality." In this verse Paul very clearly was speaking about God's expectations for humanity, not merely his sovereign rule over all things.

So the question remains: In what sense is Jesus teaching us about the will of God in the Lord's Prayer? Is Jesus asking that God's sovereign will be done on earth as it is in heaven, or is he referring to his revealed will?

He cannot be speaking of God's sovereign will because God's will is already done in heaven as it is on earth. As the psalmist wrote, "Whatever the LORD pleases, he does, in heaven and on earth, in the seas and all deeps" (Ps. 135:6). Jesus is clearly referring to God's revealed will. He is asking the Father to reshape the hearts of every single person such that God is obeyed and glorified by men on earth as the angels obey and glorify God in heaven.

Thus, in this petition, "Your will be done on earth as it is in heaven," Jesus is further explaining what it looks like for God's kingdom to come from heaven to earth. When the kingdom of God arrives anew and afresh in the hearts and lives of the lost, they begin to obey God from the heart, just as the angels in heaven. In this age, the age of the inaugurated kingdom, we know that reality only in part. In the coming age, the age of the consummated kingdom, we will experience that reality completely.

Praying "your will be done on earth as it is in heaven" also reorients our own sense of personal autonomy and sense of control over our own lives and situations. This petition causes us to forfeit all our personal claims of lordship and sovereignty over our lives. This petition expresses a humble resignation to and desire for the reign and rule of God. It is no longer "my will" that is preeminent, but his. As J. I. Packer noted, "Here more clearly than anywhere the purpose of prayer becomes plain: not to make God do my will (which is practicing magic), but to bring my will into line with his (which is what it means to practice true religion)."[4]

WHAT ARE WE REALLY ASKING?

Now we can see why this pair of petitions is so radical. By asking for the kingdom of God to come, Jesus subversively overthrows the kingdoms of man and the powers of Satan. He petitions God to create an ultimate allegiance in the hearts of all men to the true king of creation. For the kingdom of God to come means that all other kingdoms (including our own!) must fade into oblivion.

As many scholars have noted, "kingdom language" always represents a subversion of an established order. Any time a new kingdom arrives, it must do so as a rival of the current reigning powers. Writing in the last century, George Arthur Buttrick attested to this fact, noting that modern man does not like the word *kingdom*. "It savors of totalitarianism," he said.[5] Of course, what Buttrick recognized is that the carnal heart of man refuses to be ruled by anyone but himself. In the modern era we have domesticated our kings and turned them into little more than tabloid figures or national mascots. In many constitutional monarchies, the monarch only bears the responsibilities of opening parliament and adorning postage stamps.

But true kingship is not as facile or impotent. The reign of Christ is the reign of a true king: one who demands allegiance; one who will disrupt the order of our lives; one who will call us to abandon our own pursuits for the sake of his. Thus when we pray "your kingdom come," we are praying something incredibly dangerous because it imperils our comfort and devalues our ease. By praying "your kingdom come," Jesus teaches us that we are ultimately meant to value God's agenda, not our own. By making God's kingdom paramount in our hearts, we are setting aside our own paltry attempts at personal glory to pursue the glory of King Jesus.

One of the reasons we must pray for God to advance his kingdom is because we, in and of ourselves, cannot cause the kingdom to come. In fact, only the sovereign grace of God has the power to break through the darkness and establish his reign by changing the hearts of rebellious sinners. The human heart is naturally hostile to the kingdom of God because it challenges our sense of identity and commitment to self-glorification. As Augustine noted, the citizens of the City of Man are animated by self-love. They refuse and resist God's kingdom because it doesn't conform to their agenda.

Church history provides enormous insight and encouragement. The early church's proclamation of the arrival of God's kingdom in Jesus Christ was in direct confrontation with the emperor worship of the Roman cult. To declare "Jesus Christ is Lord" was to declare that Caesar was not. Thus to preach the kingdom was an act of subversion. This Christian commitment to the lordship of Christ in the arrival of God's kingdom was thus the primary reason Christians were persecuted and put to death. Christians were considered subversive and traitorous because they did not join the Imperial cult or accept the deity of Caesar.

Notably, a similar situation emerged in Nazi Germany in the first half of the twentieth century. In 1922 public Christianity was the norm in Germany. *Kulturprotestantismus*, what we might call cultural Christianity, characterized much of public life. Yet by 1942 the Nazi regime had supplanted the old cultural Christianity with a new religion: the German Evangelical Church (emphasis on *German*) under the oversight of the *Reichsbischofs*. This new state church, controlled by and therefore in support of the Nazi regime, recognized the statement "Jesus is Lord" as subversive to the state. To declare Jesus is Lord was to say Hitler was not. As a result, believers in the Confessing Church (those who refused to be incorporated into the pro-Nazi state church) could find themselves on a train to Flossenbürg or some other concentration camp for such treason.

The rapid disappearance of cultural Christianity in our own time will mean that Christians may soon find themselves in a situation similar to that of the early church in Rome or the Confessing Church in Nazi Germany. Praying for the coming of God's kingdom will be considered culturally and politically subversive.

Confessing Christ is king and expecting his kingdom to come in power will lead to direct confrontation with the culture.

Ultimately, the radical nature of this petition challenges everyone in every theological tradition. We are all guilty of trying to domesticate the kingdom so that it doesn't subvert our values or disorder our commitments. In fact, this isn't just a problem for some theological traditions. Both theological liberals and conservatives are guilty of trying to domesticate the kingdom.

For decades theological liberals and revisionist theologians have sought to speak of God's kingdom as something we can engineer through humanitarian efforts and good works. In this conception of the kingdom, God is little more than a cheerleader encouraging our own efforts. He is not one who is infinitely sovereign, but instead just someone who is infinitely resourceful. His kingdom makes no demands on our lives because, as king, he is merely an impotent monarch who simply encourages humanity to live up to its full potential.

Of course, conservatives can similarly domesticate God's kingdom by confusing a particular political party or a particular government with the kingdom. Christians too often fall prey to the temptation—as old as the Roman emperor Constantine—that we can bring about the kingdom of God by political force or some other sociological means. But God's kingdom is not of this world. As Jesus teaches us in this prayer, we are dependent on God and God alone to bring the kingdom to every heart and every corner of the earth. We cannot manufacture God's kingdom by our own efforts. Instead, we are called to be faithful in the Great Commission, trusting that God by his sovereign, supernatural grace will spread his redemptive reign to every tribe, tongue, and nation.

So what are we asking when we say "your kingdom come"? We are asking for something wonderful and something dangerous all at the same time.

- We are praying that history would be brought to a close.
- We are praying to see all the nations rejoice in the glory of God.
- We are praying to see Christ honored as king in every human heart.
- We are praying to see Satan bound, evil vanquished, death no more.
- We are praying to see the mercy of God demonstrated in the full justification and acquittal of sinners through the shed blood of the crucified and resurrected Christ.
- We are praying to see the wrath of God poured out upon sin.
- We are praying to see every knee bow and every tongue confess that Jesus Christ is Lord to the glory of God the Father.
- We are praying to see a New Jerusalem, a new heaven, and a new earth, a new creation.

This is indeed a radical prayer. We must not take this petition lightly. But, as we have seen, this petition also carries great hope. Our God will come to save us and bring us to know the fullness of his grace in the final revelation of his kingdom. To that end, we pray.

CHAPTER 5

GIVE US THIS DAY

GOD'S ABUNDANT PHYSICAL PROVISIONS

MATTHEW 6:11

In his magisterial work *The Institutes of the Christian Religion*, the sixteenth-century reformer John Calvin remarked that we can never truly know ourselves without first coming to know the character of God. As Calvin famously stated, "It is certain that man never achieves a clear knowledge of himself unless he has first looked upon God's face, and then descends from contemplating him to scrutinize himself."[1] God is our starting point in every theological and spiritual endeavor. God's character and glory are our first frame of reference.

Up to this point, the Lord's Prayer has revealed a great deal about the character of God. We have seen that for those who are in Christ, God is a caring Father. Jesus emphasized God's transcendence and omnipotence by observing that he is "in heaven." He established the worth of God and the value of his glory by teaching that God's name should be hallowed. Finally, Jesus emphasizes that God is king—the sovereign Lord who will bring his kingdom to every corner of the earth.

Indeed, the first lines of the Lord's Prayer paint an awesome portrait of God. In light of these truths, Jesus' subsequent turn to consider our own needs—"Give us this day our daily bread"—serves as a clear and unmistakable reminder that we are merely creatures; God is the creator. We are needy; God is the provider.

God has designed humans to be dependent. From the moment of birth, we rely on the kindness of others to meet our needs. We need our parents to feed us, dress us, and even train us to sleep. Even as we grow older, we remain tremendously needy. We depend on others for relationships. We need communities in which to live and work. We depend on the government for safety and security. In other words, there is no such thing as the "self-made man." We have no sufficiency in and of ourselves, and we delude ourselves by believing we can be truly independent of others. Luther once reminisced that our physical needs remind us that we are but creatures composed of dirt. Our lives are frail, fragile, and wholly dependent on the goodness of God.

The petition "give us this day our daily bread" reminds us of our dependence on God for even the most fundamental needs of life. The contrast with the depiction of God given earlier in the prayer is striking. He is glorious, hallowed, in heaven, and omnipotent.

We, on the other hand, are incapable of even getting basic sustenance without his help. In these words, then, Jesus teaches us to exalt God while humbling ourselves. The radical God-centeredness of the prayer continues. Man's pride has no place before the throne of God.

PHYSICAL NEEDS IN BIBLICAL PERSPECTIVE

We are dependent on God. Even prior to the fall, humans needed God to provide for them. Adam needed God to provide Eve to fulfill his need for a relationship. Adam and Eve could tend the garden, but only God could make it grow. Sin did not create our dependence; we are dependent simply because we are creatures.

Even though Adam and Eve were dependent before the fall, their only experience was one of surplus and abundance. They never knew a day of scarcity. After the fall, however, their experience was quite different, as is ours today. Our default experience is no longer abundance but scarcity. Food must be produced by the sweat of our brow, and its existence is never certain. Thus, after the fall we become even more dependent on God for our daily sustenance. We are no longer merely creatures in need of provision; we are sinners in need of the Creator's mercy.

In Christ we come to understand the character of God, and we can be confident that God will provide for us. As Jesus teaches us in this very prayer, God is our heavenly "Father." As a Father, he cares about our physical needs. Jesus reiterated this point in Matthew 7:9–11:

> Or which one of you, if his son asks him for bread, will give him a stone? Or if he asks for a fish, will give him a serpent? If you then, who are evil, know how to give good gifts to your children, how much more will your Father who is in heaven give good things to those who ask him!

THE DIGNITY OF THE BODY AND OF PHYSICAL NEEDS

Jesus' focus up to this point in the Lord's Prayer has been on the greatness and grandeur of God, yet with the words "give us this day our daily bread," he moves from the clouds of heaven to the trials and troubles of our own dusty streets and dirty kitchens. He profoundly rejects any view that devalues the body or sees physical needs as somehow unspiritual or even sinful. Paul referred to people with such views as those "who forbid marriage and require abstinence from foods that God created to be received with thanksgiving by those who believe and know the truth" (1 Tim. 4:3).

We need not be surprised by the earthiness of Jesus' prayer here. The Father cares not only for great things, such as advancing his kingdom in the world, but also for small things, such as feeding his children. Further, Jesus shows us that all of life must be lived before the face of God. Our lives are not divided between spiritual activities and earthly activities. Rather, every activity must be lived for the glory of God. Even our appetites are to be brought before the throne of grace. J. I. Packer expressed this point quite beautifully:

> The Bible opposes all long-faced asceticism by saying that if you enjoy health, good appetite, physical agility, and marriage in the sense that you have been given them, you should enjoy them in the further sense of delighting in them. Such delight is (not the whole, but) part of our duty and our service of God, for without it we are being simply ungrateful for good gifts. As Screwtape truly said (with disgust), "He's a hedonist at heart": God values pleasure, and it is his pleasure to give pleasure. Well did some rabbis teach that at the judgment God will hold against us every pleasure that he offered us and we neglected. Do we yet know how to enjoy ourselves—yes, physically too—to the glory of God?[2]

Regrettably, we often do not recognize just how dignified our physical needs are until we witness true deprivation and scarcity. German theologian Helmut Thielicke once described the horrors of World War II and explained that one of the most terrible realities of the war was widespread deprivation and starvation. He reminded his readers that we should never undervalue physical needs, observing that a hyper-spiritual theology that ignores physical needs has never had to come face-to-face with the horrors of deprivation. Thielicke is right. Those who believe providing for or praying for physical needs is somehow undignified have never witnessed refugees fleeing from a war zone with nothing more than the clothes on their back.[3]

Jesus dignifies our physical needs by teaching us to petition God on matters as seemingly insignificant as the food on our plate. You may have heard the following quote, often attributed to Samuel Johnson, "He who would deny the stomach will soon be thinking of nothing but the stomach." As we all know, the more we try to deny the necessity of food, the more urgent the need becomes.

God created us as embodied creatures with physical needs such as food, water, and shelter. Furthermore, he even gave his benediction over the physical world when he called everything that he had made good.

Food, rightly received, functions as a constant reminder of the greatness of God and our need for his goodness and provision. Unlike us, God will never grow hungry or need sustenance. Humans on the other hand are in need of constant provision. God made us this way so that we would rely on his providence and kindness, regularly remembering that we are not master of our own fate—only he is. As the old hymn reminds us, "I need thee every hour." Our hunger serves as a reminder of that truth several times a day.

Jesus highlights our regular dependence on God by teaching us to pray for our "daily" bread. This word shows us that we ought not pray for opulence and riches, only for the needs of the day. Further, this word teaches us to pray for our needs every day, seeking God's provision in our life hour by hour. In sum, the word *daily* here teaches us to train our hearts to depend consistently on God, rather than just in times of need.

AN OLD TESTAMENT ILLUSTRATION

The account of Israel wandering in the wilderness provides a helpful illustration of just how God cares for the daily needs of his people. In Exodus 16:4–7, the Lord told Moses that he would provide bread from heaven with the requirement that they gather only enough to meet their needs for that day, except, of course, the double portion gathered on Saturday to prevent work on the Sabbath. The Lord intended for the Israelites to gather a day's portion to "test them" (Ex. 16:4). Even in the wilderness we see the Lord teaching his people to depend on him for daily provision for the most basic needs and, of course, to not rely on themselves.

Yet, even as the Israelites grumbled against God's provision of bread, he continued to graciously provide for them. Exodus 16:11–18 states that in the evening, quail "covered the camp," and in the morning the people would be filled with bread. Verses 17–18 indicate that God's provision was perfect for each person who had gathered bread. As verse 18 says, "Whoever gathered much had nothing left over, and whoever gathered little had no lack. Each of them gathered as much as he could eat."

These passages point to God's loving, gracious provision for his people—even for a people characterized by sin and grumbling. The final words attest to the character of God's provision: "Whoever gathered much had nothing left over, and whoever gathered little had no lack." In other words, God's provision for each family was according to its need. God's provision was perfectly sufficient in each and every case.

The same is true for God's new covenant people today. We may never experience great riches, but we can be confident that God will provide for us—though sometimes his perception of what we most need may be different from our own. As Israel stood at the edge of Canaan after forty years of wandering, Moses was able to look at the congregation and say, "Your clothing did not wear out on you and your foot did not swell these forty years" (Deut. 8:4). Not only did God's provision meet the needs of the day, he met the needs of *every* day of the journey. Like the Israelites, when we finally enter into the heavenly Canaan we will be able to look back over the course of our lives and affirm these same truths. At times God may not provide for us in the way that *we think* is best. But we will always find that he provides for us according to his infinite love and care.

BREAD OF EARTH, BREAD FROM HEAVEN: ECHOES OF ETERNITY IN JESUS' PETITION FOR BREAD

Before leaving this request we should note that, in a tangential way, this request also reminds us of our daily need for the Lord Jesus. Moses reminded the Israelites in Deuteronomy 8:3 that the reason God let the

Israelites go hungry for a time before providing them with manna was so that they might learn that "man does not live by bread alone, but man lives by every word that comes from the mouth of the LORD." This passage teaches us that God designed physical needs to point to our deeper spiritual needs. Our need for daily physical sustenance is a faint echo of our daily need of spiritual sustenance and satisfaction from God. This was true for ancient Israel and is true for Christians today. The only way that we will taste the goodness of God's provision is by living according to what comes from the mouth of God.

This is why Jesus regularly referred to himself as the "bread of life," the true manna sent from heaven (John 6:35). He is God's ultimate provision for our spiritual lives. Each day, as we pray for our daily bread, we should be reminded of our daily need for Christ to forgive our sins and empower us for obedience. Each time we pray for daily bread, we should recognize our deeper need for the bread of life—the only one who can truly satisfy.

CHAPTER 6

FORGIVE US OUR DEBTS

THE PRAYER OF GOD'S
NEW COVENANT PEOPLE

MATTHEW 6:12

THE GOSPEL FOUNDATION OF
THE LORD'S PRAYER

We are a nation of debtors. Millions of young people are on the verge of bankruptcy with unpayable credit card debt that compounds yet more interest every month. The problem of school debt, often running into the hundreds of thousands of dollars, has now become a national crisis. Even the federal government is in debt—debt that has soared into untold trillions of dollars.

Yet while many Americans view debt as an annoyance, in the ancient world debt was punishable by prison sentence. In the Roman Empire, prisons were not generally filled with criminals; they were populated with debtors. Most convicted criminals were executed or were forced to serve some other form of punishment for their crimes, but those who could not make good on their payments were incarcerated until they could pay what they owed. This system was meant to put pressure on the families of the incarcerated debtor to find the necessary money to pay their debts to free their loved one from prison.

In the Roman Empire, then, debt typically meant severe pain and tragedy for an individual and a family. In our day we experience frustration and anxiety with debt, but in the days of Jesus, debt was a matter of life and death. This is the context in which Jesus teaches us to pray "forgive us our debts, as we also have forgiven our debtors." Jesus' use of the word *debts* is meant to evoke in our mind both a serious offense and a corresponding serious punishment. To be forgiven a debt was no mere trifle, but an act of extravagant mercy.

If the petition "give us this day our daily bread" emphasizes our most urgent physical needs, the petition "forgive us our debts" emphasizes our most urgent spiritual need. Saying we owe a debt to God means that we have failed to give him the obedience he is rightly due. We owe God our obedience, and we have failed to pay up. Thus, as sinners, we stand before God condemned, rightly deserving his just wrath. Only God's forgiveness can clear our guilt and establish a meaningful relationship between God and us.

This petition reminds us that the Lord's Prayer is not a casual prayer for the generically religious. This prayer is a gospel prayer. We can only say these words and ask these things of God when we stand on the finished, atoning work of Jesus Christ. Indeed, this petition demonstrates that the theological bedrock of the Lord's Prayer is nothing less than the gospel. We can only rightly pray the Lord's Prayer when we recognize that we are deeply sinful and only God's grace in Christ can remedy our souls.

GETTING THE GOSPEL RIGHT

The logic of this particular petition in the Lord's Prayer has been misconstrued so often that we would do well to remind ourselves of what Scripture teaches about the gospel. Nothing is more central to the message of Scripture than the gospel. If we err on this point, we err on all others. Many interpreters believe that Jesus is saying that God only forgives us when we *earn* his forgiveness through forgiving others. Nothing could be further from the truth. In fact, this petition does not say "forgive us our debts *because* we forgive our debtors," but "forgive us our debts *as* we have forgiven our debtors." The difference between those two phrases, as we shall see, is the difference between the gospel of Jesus Christ and no gospel at all.

The sum and substance of the gospel is that a holy and righteous God who must claim a full penalty for our sin both *demands* that penalty and *provides* it. His self-substitution is Jesus Christ the Son, whose perfect obedience and perfectly accomplished atonement on the cross purchased all that is necessary for our salvation. Jesus Christ met the full demands of the righteousness and justice of God against our sin.

Paul summarized the work of Christ in 2 Corinthians 5:21: "For our sake he made him to be sin who knew no sin, so that in him we might become the righteousness of God." Christ is our substitute and his life is sacrificed for our sin so that God's wrath against us is removed.

How then do we benefit from the sacrifice of Christ for us? Paul answered that we do not earn the righteousness of God in Christ; instead it is given to us freely when we believe the gospel: "For all have sinned and fall short of the glory of God, and are justified by his grace as a gift, through the redemption that is in Christ Jesus" (Rom. 3:23–24). Indeed, nothing in us or achieved by us is the grounds of our acceptance with God. Instead, as Paul made clear, "To the one who does not work but believes in him who justifies the ungodly, his faith is counted as righteousness" (Rom. 4:5).

The gospel humbles all human pride and destroys any notion of self-righteousness. We do not come before the throne of grace presenting our so-called good works to God. Instead, we cling to the sacrifice and righteousness of Christ with the empty hand of faith. As the old hymn "Rock of Ages" states, "Nothing in my hands I bring, simply to the cross I cling."

Yet, once we believe in Christ, we no longer live and act as we did before trusting in him. True conversion is marked by lifelong repentance and a new life of holiness. Not only does God forgive us of our sins, but he also gives us a new life that responds to his Word and has new desires for the things of God. As the author of

Hebrews reminded us, once we are included in the new covenant, God writes his law on our minds and on our hearts (Heb. 8:10) and even puts his Spirit within us (Ezek. 36:26). Good works always accompany true salvation, but they are the fruit of salvation, not the root of salvation.

In theological terms, sanctification *always* follows justification. This means that when God saves a sinner, he will always conform that person into the image of Christ (Rom. 8:28–30). Paul summarized this comprehensive portrait of the gospel in Ephesians 2:8–10:

> For by grace you have been saved through faith. And this is not your own doing; it is the gift of God, not a result of works, so that no one may boast. For we are his workmanship, created in Christ Jesus for good works, which God prepared beforehand, that we should walk in them.

The apostle was very clear. We are saved by faith alone in the work of Christ. All this comes from the grace of God. But we are not freed just from the penalty of sin; we are also freed from the power of sin. While our salvation is not a "result of works," Paul noted that it does result *in* works, ones that God himself prepared for us to do. The portrait of the gospel is indeed astounding. We are saved by grace alone through faith alone in Christ alone, which then results in our being transformed into the image of Christ (2 Cor. 3:18). Indeed the whole of our salvation proclaims the ineffable glory of God.

THE GOSPEL THEOLOGY OF
"FORGIVE US OUR DEBTS"

The petition "forgive us our debts as we forgive our debtors" summarizes all the theology in the section above. This request is a gospel primer in miniature. First, this prayer establishes that we are sinners in need of forgiveness. Jesus identifies that our deepest, most urgent spiritual problem is nothing less than personal rebellion against a holy God. Our fundamental spiritual problem is not a lack of education, lack of opportunity, an inability to express ourselves, or unmet social needs. Our problem is sin. We have transgressed God's law and spurned his commandments. As a result, we need his forgiveness.

Second, Jesus teaches us not only that we have sinned but also that we have the hope of forgiveness. It is easy to miss just how audacious the words of Jesus actually are. Jesus is teaching sinners, rebels against God, to have the audacity to approach God's throne—a throne established in justice and holiness—and ask for forgiveness. The only thing that can account for this boldness is the gospel of Jesus Christ. Only the work of Christ on behalf of sinners could possibly enable a sinner to go before God's holy throne to petition that God forgive his debts. Only those with hearts fixed on the Lord Jesus Christ and his atoning work on the cross can appeal to God's mercy and redemption.

Third, we see in this passage that God is willing to forgive sin. By teaching us to pray in this way, Jesus implies that God desires to forgive our sin. Scripture repeatedly makes this point:

> [God] desires all people to be saved and to come to the knowledge of the truth. (1 Tim. 2:4)

> The Lord is not slow to fulfill his promise as some count slowness, but is patient toward you, not wishing that any should perish, but that all should reach repentance. (2 Peter 3:9)

> Have I any pleasure in the death of the wicked, declares the Lord God, and not rather that he should turn from his way and live? (Ezek. 18:23)

Indeed, the only thing that surpasses our constant need for forgiveness is God's determination to forgive sin. As the puritan Richard Sibbes famously said, "There is more mercy in Christ than sin in us."[1] Sibbes's pithy maxim is nothing more than a summary of the teaching of the apostles. The apostle John made this same point in his first epistle:

> If we say we have no sin, we deceive ourselves, and the truth is not in us. If we confess our sins, he is faithful and just to forgive us our sins and to cleanse us from all unrighteousness. If we say we have not sinned, we make him a liar, and his word is not in us. (1 John 1:8–10)

Finally, this petition demonstrates the relational character of the kingdom of God. The Lord's Prayer is ultimately about the arrival of God's kingdom and about the character of its members. This petition is yet another reminder that the kingdom of Christ is radically unlike the kingdoms of this world. The citizens of earthly kingdoms are committed first and foremost to themselves and to their own power, and are characterized by selfish ambition, self-promotion, and cruelty. True forgiveness has no real foothold in the kingdoms of man. But citizens of God's kingdom are characterized by mercy, kindness, compassion, and forgiveness. We are included in God's kingdom only by his act of forgiving us and, as a result, we are those who forgive one another—even when we might want to do otherwise. The kingdom of God is no place for malice and unchecked bitterness. The King himself makes us citizens by forgiving us, and thus the kingdom's citizens forgive one another.

If you have ever been tempted to think that the gospel is nowhere present in the Lord's Prayer, think again! This petition only makes sense in the context of Christ's provision for us. By agreeing with God that we are sinners and repenting of that sin by asking for forgiveness, God clears our debts on account of Christ's work for us.

If this does not shock us, then we have grown far too familiar with the gospel and the glory of God's grace. The extravagant mercy of God shown in this petition should be on our lips and in our hearts daily. When we recognize we are debtors, then we see ourselves as we truly are, beggars at the throne of grace. Martin Luther, the great Reformer of the sixteenth century, certainly understood and reveled in this truth. When Luther came to die, his last moments were characterized by delirium and moving in and out of consciousness. Yet in one last moment of clarity Luther said (mixing German with Latin), *"Wir sind bettler. Hoc est verum"*—We are beggars, this is true.

FROM FORGIVEN TO FORGIVING: THE TRANSFORMATIVE POWER OF GOD'S FORGIVENESS

Not only does Jesus teach us to petition God for forgiveness, he also teaches us to pray that God forgive us *in the same way* that we forgive our debtors. Now we must be very careful with this clause so that we don't take it to mean something that Jesus would not affirm. Jesus is decidedly not saying that we are forgiven by God *because* we have forgiven other people. That would make the grounds of our acceptance with God our own works and not God's grace. Scripture is very clear that we are justified before God by faith alone, not by works of the law.

What Jesus is affirming in these words is that when we experience God's forgiveness, we are fundamentally transformed into forgiving people. In other words, one way we can know if we have experienced God's forgiveness is to see if we have become a forgiving people. It is simply impossible to experience the richness of God's grace and remain a stubborn, obstinate, coldhearted person. Those who truly know the forgiveness of sins, forgive others.

Jesus emphasized this point a number of times throughout his ministry:

> Then Peter came up and said to him, "Lord, how often will my brother sin against me, and I forgive him? As many as seven times?" Jesus said to him, "I do not say to you seven times, but seventy-seven times." (Matt. 18:21–22)

> Judge not, and you will not be judged; condemn not, and you will not be condemned; forgive, and you will be forgiven. (Luke 6:37)

> Pay attention to yourselves! If your brother sins, rebuke him, and if he repents, forgive him, and if he sins against you seven times in the day, and turns to you seven times, saying, "I repent," you must forgive him. (Luke 17:3–4)

In fact, one of Jesus' most well-known parables, the parable of the unforgiving servant, focuses on the principle of forgiveness and specifically delineates why those who have been forgiven are themselves forgiving.

> The kingdom of heaven may be compared to a king who wished to settle accounts with his servants. When he began to settle, one was brought to him who owed him ten thousand talents. And since he could not pay, his master ordered him to be sold, with his wife and children and all that he had, and payment to be made. So the servant fell on his knees, imploring him, "Have

patience with me, and I will pay you everything." And out of pity for him, the master of that servant released him and forgave him the debt. But when that same servant went out, he found one of his fellow servants who owed him a hundred denarii, and seizing him, he began to choke him, saying, "Pay what you owe." So his fellow servant fell down and pleaded with him, "Have patience with me, and I will pay you." He refused and went and put him in prison until he should pay the debt. When his fellow servants saw what had taken place, they were greatly distressed, and they went and reported to their master all that had taken place. Then his master summoned him and said to him, "You wicked servant! I forgave you all that debt because you pleaded with me. And should not you have had mercy on your fellow servant, as I had mercy on you?" And in anger his master delivered him to the jailers, until he should pay all his debt. So also my heavenly Father will do to every one of you, if you do not forgive your brother from your heart. (Matt. 18:23–35)

Jesus' words on forgiveness are clear. Without forgiving others we will not be forgiven. Again, the grounds of our forgiveness is never our own works. But forgiveness is a necessary evidence that we have received forgiveness. If we do not forgive, we will not be forgiven. Hard hearts have no place in the kingdom of God. The reason, of course, is that the King himself is a forgiving king. Just as he forgives us when we rebel against him, so the citizens of God's kingdom forgive one another.

CHAPTER 7

LEAD US NOT INTO TEMPTATION

FIGHTING THE ENEMY THROUGH PRAYER

MATTHEW 6:13

When I was a child, I loved camping. For twelve-year-old boys, camping trips have many thrilling aspects, among them that you could spend an entire day outside without being chaperoned by your mom. I vividly remember how my father helped me get ready for camping trips. He would pack Vienna Sausages, canned baked beans, and oatmeal cookies. This was an ideal diet for a twelve-year-old boy.

On one particular trip, I remember playing with friends in an abandoned palmetto field. We ran ourselves into exhaustion, which I now realize was the scoutmaster's plan. After a long day, we finally crawled into our tents and fell asleep. The next morning we were awakened by three gunshots. Racing out of our tents, we found Colonel Mack Geiger, one of the leading laymen of the church, draping three enormous diamondback rattlesnakes across the front of his jeep. When we asked where he had shot them, he pointed to the bushes—the very palmetto bushes we had been playing near the night before, blissfully unaware of the danger so near.

THE ILLUSION OF ENEMY-LESS CHRISTIAN DISCIPLESHIP

We like to think the world is a safe place, but it is not. The world is a tremendously dangerous place. We like to imagine that evil is distant but, as the headlines reveal, evil is always lurking near. Even when we don't see any enemies, invisible threats like germs, viruses, bacteria, and toxins surround us. If we are honest, we know that danger can crop up in any circumstance.

Christians should recognize this truth particularly when it comes to our spiritual lives. The Bible clearly teaches that the Devil and his demons are real and that these invisible enemies are bent on destroying our spiritual lives. Yet many evangelicals rarely, if ever, meditate on or live in light of this truth. Some Christians avoid any discussion of demonic forces because they are overreacting to fanatics who obsess over evil spirits and see the Devil in everything. Still other Christians fear that if we start to talk too much about the Devil, we will inevitably undermine personal responsibility in our sin.

C. S. Lewis observed the same phenomenon in his

classic work *The Screwtape Letters*. As Lewis explained, humanity is prone to two extremes when it comes to thinking about demonic forces.

> There are two equal and opposite errors into which our race can fall about the devils. One is to disbelieve in their existence. The other is to believe, and to feel an excessive and unhealthy interest in them. They themselves are equally pleased by both errors and hail a materialist or a magician with the same delight.[1]

The aim of this chapter is to fall into neither of these ditches. Certainly the Devil and his demons are not behind every corner of our lives and responsible for every negative spiritual thing that happens. Yet at the same time, the Bible clearly warns us about demonic powers and encourages us to remain diligently opposed to their influence.

Regrettably, many Christians are blissfully complacent in matters of spiritual warfare. If Christians truly embraced biblical teaching on demonic powers, we would come to church with a tremendous sense of the fact that God has rescued us from the domain of darkness. As Søren Kierkegaard observed of the Danish church in his generation, most people sit in church, listen with their hands folded over their stomachs, and direct their sleepy eyes slightly upward.[2] Rather than celebrating their redemption from the domain of darkness and living in light of this truth, they are indifferent to the fight. Jesus' final petition reminds us that we have a daily fight against principalities and powers: "lead us not into temptation, but deliver us from evil."

WHY WE NEED THIS PETITION

Jesus' reminder to pray regularly against temptation reminds us just how prevalent and dangerous the appeal of sin can be in the Christian life. Once again the issue of kingdom and kingship is front and center. Sin and temptation are harsh masters. As the story of Cain reminds us, sin doesn't just want to play a minor role in our lives; it wants to "rule" over us (Gen. 4:7). Asking to be delivered from sin and temptation is a cry that emerges only from the heart of a citizen of God's kingdom. We desire to submit to the rule and reign of God, not the dominion of sin. This petition is one of kingdom warfare, asking that God conquer the powers of sin, Satan, and the demons so that we might live for his heavenly kingdom.

This petition also reminds us of several other very important points. First, Christians must recognize that temptations are a real and daily threat to communion with God and life with Christ. The most dangerous thing a Christian can ever do is believe that he is somehow immune to temptation. In fact, failing to account for the dangers of temptation betrays a severe misunderstanding of the gospel. In the gospel we come to recognize both the depravity of our hearts and the freedom of God's grace in Christ. If we, at any point, think that we are somehow freed up from fighting temptation, then we have both overestimated our own spiritual state and grossly underestimated our need for God's grace.

Second, this petition reminds us that we are not able to resist temptation by our own power. Most people know by experience that our willpower is not quite as strong as we would like to think. Anyone who has ever struggled to keep up with a diet plan knows just how weak-willed we can be. Even as we work to achieve our goals through sheer willpower, we find ourselves incapable of willing more willpower!

The gospel, however, and this petition in the Lord's Prayer turn our attention away from our own strength to the strength of another. Jesus does not teach us to pray, "Lord, give me more willpower in the fight against sin." He teaches us to ask for shepherding and deliverance—"Lead us not into temptation, but deliver us from evil." These words express a heart of dependence, not self-sufficiency.

In fact, consider the phrase "deliver us." These are words of desperation and powerlessness, not self-sufficiency. Jesus does not teach us to pray that God might "help a bit" or "give strength." We do not meet God halfway and trust him to do the rest. Rather, God does it all! He is the deliverer; we are the delivered. He is the savior; we are the saved. The Bible does not teach that God helps those who help themselves; instead, God helps those who are at the end of themselves. The gospel teaches that only by God's grace can we truly overcome the temptations of the world, the wickedness of our own hearts, and the power of the Devil.

Third, Christians must pray for endurance in the fight against temptation. Remember, Jesus is giving us a model prayer, which means these are the *types* of petitions that should characterize our prayer life every day. Christians should pray this petition as well as pray for the grace to overcome temptation all the way to the grave.

DOES GOD LEAD PEOPLE INTO TEMPTATION?

This petition immediately sparks a very important question: Does God lead us into temptation? The Lord's Prayer might seem to imply that there are times when God does in fact lead us into temptation. Yet when we let Scripture interpret Scripture, we find that God does not tempt his people. James, for instance, explained that God does not lead us into temptation or seduce his people to sin: "Let no one say when he is tempted, 'I am being tempted by God,' for God cannot be tempted with evil and he himself tempts no one" (James 1:13).

As James made clear, no evil exists in God. The Lord is not demanding our holiness while also tempting us to fail. God takes no delight in our sin. He is not playing a cruel game with us. He does not push us to the brink of sin just to see if we will fall over the edge.

So when Jesus prays "lead us not into temptation," he is not asking God to act in a way contrary to his nature, but in a way entirely consistent with his holiness. Jesus is asking God to lead him away from evil and away from the lusts of his own flesh.

But we must also recognize that while God will never *tempt* us, he may sometimes *test* us in order to strengthen our faith. Again, as James wrote: "Count it all joy, my brothers, when you meet trials of various kinds, for you know that the testing of your faith produces steadfastness. And let steadfastness have its full effect that you may be perfect and complete, lacking in nothing" (James 1:2–4). So God does test us, but he does not seek to tempt us into sin.

We can often confuse God's tests with temptations because our hearts often use difficult circumstances as an excuse for sinful behavior. A test is a trying circumstance or a difficult situation orchestrated in our lives by God. A temptation, however, is an invitation to sin, an encouragement to engage in something contrary to God's law. God certainly tests us, but he never tempts us. We must never allow God's tests to lead to temptations. Indeed, in the midst of trials we should pray this prayer more frequently and with more urgency than perhaps at any other point in our lives.

This petition makes several important theological points. First, we must recognize that temptations are a real, daily threat to our life with Christ. The question is not *if* we will encounter temptations, but what will we do with temptations *when* we encounter them? Until the consummation of the kingdom, our desire to sin will continually flare up and try to entice us to act in a way that dishonors the Lord.

Second, we must understand that we are not able

to resist temptation by our own power. This prayer underlines the fact that apart from God, we simply are unable to resist temptation. Apart from God's sanctifying work through the Holy Spirit, we will not be able to push back against the spiritual forces that arraign us.

Third, we must pray for endurance in the fight against temptation. If Jesus is teaching us to pray against temptation in the same way we pray for our "daily" bread, then we must recognize that the fight against sin will be a lifelong struggle. Only by regularly pleading with the Lord for strength to overcome temptation will we endure to the end.

Fourth, we must pray that the Lord delivers us from our own personal patterns of temptation. As most of us recognize, each individual Christian has a different pattern of temptation. As we pray, we should pray not only against temptation generically but against our specific temptations and enticing sins. We all have weaknesses. The adversary will exploit those weaknesses at every opportunity. This is why we need the Lord's gracious hand to guide us away from temptation at every turn.

THE ANATOMY OF TEMPTATION

Temptation can be both internal and external. With regard to internal temptation, James wrote, "Each person is tempted when he is lured and enticed by his own desire. Then desire when it has conceived gives birth to sin, and sin when it is fully grown brings forth death" (James 1:14–15).

As this passage makes clear, temptation emerges from *inside* our hearts when we are carried away by our own desires. Unless we fight against these sinful desires, these internal temptations turn into outward sins. Pride leads to arrogance. Lust leads to sexual immorality. Ultimately, we are at war with our own desires. Our greatest enemy, indwelling sin, is with us at all times.

Yet Scripture also teaches that temptations come from the outside as well. Matthew 4 provides us with one of the clearest pictures of this when the Devil tempted Jesus in the wilderness. The Devil tried to entice Jesus to sin by presenting him with appealing opportunities in exchange for worship. This is how external temptation comes to us as well. Satan and his demons appeal to our flesh and incite us to follow after sinful desires.

Truly, temptations are everywhere. The world surrounds us with a circus of temptations. In fact, our culture considers it unnatural to resist these temptations. Scripture, however, demands a clear and drastic response to temptation. Speaking hyperbolically, Jesus told his disciples,

> If your right eye causes you to sin, tear it out and throw it away. For it is better that you lose one of your members than that your whole body be thrown into hell. And if your right hand causes you to sin, cut it off and throw it away. For it is better that you lose one of your members than that your whole body go into hell. (Matt. 5:29–30)

Christians must never entertain temptation. We are to radically reject it and flee from it. The appeal of sin is the scintillating promise of joy and happiness. But we must, as Jesus teaches, ever beware of its false promises. Sin can only deliver on the promise of hell. The fact that Jesus teaches us to fight temptation with such radical language evidences his great love for us. Better we lose a hand in the fight against sin than lose our soul by giving in to sin's pleasures.

THE DEVIL MADE ME DO IT . . . REALLY?

While the final petition of the Lord's Prayer is typically rendered "deliver us from evil," most modern scholars and translations note that the most appropriate translation is probably "deliver us from *the evil one*." In other words, this is not just evil as some inanimate force, but a personal evil being—the Devil.

Many modern Christians consider themselves too sophisticated to fear the Devil. Yet Jesus teaches us that we will never combat temptation to the fullest extent until we recognize that we have an adversary that plots against our personal holiness. Satan makes sin look beautiful when its true form is infinitely ugly. He makes that which is evil look good and that which is good look evil. As Peter noted, "Be sober-minded; be watchful. Your adversary the devil prowls around like a roaring lion, seeking someone to devour" (1 Peter 5:8).

Thus, we may never make real strides against temptation until we learn our need to pray this petition. Only as we recognize that our struggle with sin is not only internal but external as well, will we be able to heed with any urgency James 4:7: "Submit yourselves therefore to God. Resist the devil, and he will flee from you."

With God's help we can overcome Satan's advances because he who is in us is more powerful than he who is in the world (1 John 4:4). Scripture clearly teaches Satan is not an anti-god in some form of theological dualism with two equally powerful forces of good and evil. He is a created being who is no match for God's wisdom and power. The book of Revelation makes this truth clear.

> Now war arose in heaven, Michael and his angels fighting against the dragon. And the dragon and his angels fought back, but he was defeated, and there was no longer any place for them in heaven. And the great dragon was thrown down, that ancient serpent, who is called the devil and Satan, the deceiver of the whole world—he was thrown down to the earth, and his angels were thrown down with him. And I heard a loud voice in heaven, saying, "Now the salvation and the power and the kingdom of our God and the authority of his Christ have come, for the accuser of our brothers has been thrown down, who accuses them day and night before our God." (12:7–10)

Satan's doom is certain. The promised Son *did* crush the serpent's head. Unfortunately, this serpent with a crushed head still has fangs and takes prisoners. But in the final day his destruction will be final and complete. As Luther said in his famous hymn "A Mighty Fortress Is Our God," "one little word shall fell him." As we await that day, Christians must not fail to recognize our constant need for deliverance from the evil one. We need to pray that we would not be found wanting. Jesus taught his disciples that the best weapon against temptation is prayer. When we do not pray faithfully, our defenses are down. Thus, the tempter has his opportunity. In the heart lacking prayer, Satan easily sows seeds of temptation.

FIGHTING THE POWERS OF DARKNESS IN THE LIFE OF THE CHURCH

As Paul noted, when we are delivered from Satan's clutches, we are transferred out of the kingdom of darkness into the kingdom of God's dear Son (Col. 1:13). But note, we are transferred into a kingdom—a kingdom made visible by local congregations who gather in the name of the Lord to share in one another's lives and in the work of the ministry. This is why Jesus teaches us to pray in the plural, "deliver *us* from evil."

Every Christian church is supposed to be a deliverance ministry. Christians are in this together. We cannot be faithful individually if we are not faithful together. The author of Hebrews understood the importance of the Christian community in this regard:

Let us hold fast the confession of our hope without wavering, for he who promised is faithful. And let us consider how to stir up one another to love and good works, not neglecting to meet together, as is the habit of some, but encouraging one another, and all the more as you see the Day drawing near. (Heb. 10:23–25)

Part of the protection against sin that the Lord has given us is being together. Together we hear the Word of God, pray, sing, take the Lord's Supper, celebrate baptism, and hold one another accountable. The Lord uses the local church made up of Christians walking in holiness to keep his people from temptation, sin, and the power of the evil one.

CONCLUSION

After that fateful camping trip, I never went out into the Everglades the same way. I still played in the palmetto fields, of course, but I went with eyes opened to the dangers that were lurking in the bushes. In the same way, Christians should recognize that spiritual danger surrounds us.

Temptation comes to individuals, churches, and institutions. We know the power of temptation by looking in both history books and the mirror. If we are honest with ourselves, we are not up to the task. But Jesus teaches us that we have access to deliverance from sin and temptation by the grace and mercy of God, which is why we must repeatedly pray this prayer of deliverance. We are frail in our flesh and must pray for God's protection from evil. As the familiar hymn

"O Worship the King" reminds us: "Frail children of dust and feeble as frail, in thee do we trust, nor find thee to fail; thy mercies how tender, how firm to the end, our maker, defender, redeemer, and friend."

EPILOGUE

THINE IS THE KINGDOM

MATTHEW 6:13

Many Christians who regularly say the Lord's Prayer in church services each week or remember a version they memorized as a child recite concluding words that do not appear in many modern translations—"for yours is the kingdom and the power and the glory forever, Amen." The reason these words are not found in modern translations such as the NIV or the ESV is that they probably did not appear in the original copy of Matthew. As a result of studying ancient manuscripts, scholars now believe with some certainty that these words were probably a later addition to the Lord's Prayer. Since the Lord's Prayer seems to end rather abruptly, Christians in the early church added a doxology to the end of the prayer so as to give God the final word of praise in corporate worship settings.

Is it right or wrong to append these words to the

Lord's Prayer? It would certainly be wrong to ignore the textual evidence and assert that these words are scriptural and part of Matthew's Gospel. We should never say something is part of Scripture that the author never intended. At the same time, it is not wrong to recite the Lord's Prayer with the concluding doxology or to benefit from this tradition—so long as we understand the words are not themselves Scripture. The reasons for this are numerous.

First, doxologies are found all throughout Scripture. In fact, one of the doxologies found in the Old Testament looks almost exactly like the doxology traditionally appended to the Lord's Prayer: "Yours, O LORD, is the greatness and the power and the glory and the victory and the majesty, for all that is in the heavens and in the earth is yours. Yours is the kingdom, O LORD, and you are exalted as head above all" (1 Chron. 29:11).

Additionally, the psalms provide example after example of prayers beginning in supplication and ending in doxology. And this tradition of concluding prayers with doxologies continued into the early church. One of the earliest Christian documents outside the New Testament, *The Didache*—a treatise dating from the first century—has a version of the Lord's Prayer that includes this very doxology. Simply put, doxologies are a regular part of the worship of the people of God and have a unique role in developing their piety. As J. I. Packer noted,

> Doxologies (that is, acts of praise to God for his glory) pop up all through the Bible. . . . Personal devotion

praise and prayer grow out of, lead into, and stir up each other. Need felt and need met are their respective mainsprings, and praise for what God is and does, is the strong support of hope in what he can, and will, do. . . . So the more you pray, the more matter you will have for praise.[1]

Second, doxologies are an appropriate response to the saving purposes of God and his glory. As I hope this book has shown, the Lord's Prayer clearly expresses the glory of God and the gospel of grace. It reveals the coming of the kingdom of Christ, the forgiveness provided by the King, his daily provision and care for his people, and his deliverance of his people from the powers of this age. In light of these truths, Christians should respond with effusive praise. Prayer that truly reflects the heart of God is inseparable from a response of praise. Again, as Packer explained, "Prayer and praise are like a bird's two wings: with both working, you soar; with one out of action, you are earthbound. But birds should not be earthbound, nor Christians praiseless."[2]

Third, the theology of the traditional doxology is particularly fitting with the content of the Lord's Prayer. The elements of "kingdom," "power," and "glory" are found throughout the Lord's Prayer. At the prayer's beginning, Jesus taught us to pray that God's kingdom come. The prayer also reveals God's power by showing us he is the King, the Provider, the Savior, and the Deliverer. And finally, it shows us his glory by revealing him as the Father *in heaven* whose very name is to be *hallowed* in all the earth. The traditional

doxology reminds us at the prayer's end that the kingdom will indeed come, for it belongs to the God of all
glory and power. Indeed, the doxology perfectly and
succinctly sums up the character of God as revealed in
the Lord's Prayer and does so in the posture of praise.

A FINAL ADMONITION

Every generation of Christians must learn to make the
request, like the disciples before them, "Lord, teach
us to pray." Every generation of Christians must also
remember that Jesus' response to that question now is
the same as it was two thousand years ago. If we would
have the Lord himself teach us how to pray, then we
must turn to the Lord's Prayer for instruction.

As this book has shown, each petition is a theology
lesson in itself. None of Jesus' words were careless, and
this is particularly true of the Lord's Prayer. This prayer
turned the world upside down. This prayer is dangerous, overturning the kingdom of the principalities and
powers of this world. This prayer is hopeful, expecting
the kingdom of God to come in fullness with Christ
on the throne. This prayer is compassionate, teaching
us to call God our Father and depend on him for our
every meal. This prayer is reverent, showing that nothing is more sacred than the name of God. This prayer is
good news, reminding each of us that God forgives sin
and delivers us from the powers of darkness.

In an age of superstition and superficiality, the Lord's
Prayer is a beacon of true biblical piety and theologically

informed worship. As Christians await the arrival of God's kingdom in its fullness, let us continually return to these words, asking with humble hearts, "Lord, teach us to pray."

Finally, I want to return to Martin Luther's advice to his barber. Going all the way back to the Old Testament, God's people have ended their prayers with "Amen." Why? The word signals agreement and affirmation, but it actually means much more. As Luther said to Master Peter the Barber:

> Notice, at last, that you have made the "Amen" strong every time and not doubt. God is surely listening to you with every grace and is saying yes to your prayer. Do not think to yourself that you are kneeling or standing there alone, for all Christendom, all upright Christians, are with you and you among them in a unanimous, harmonious prayer, which God cannot disdain. And do not leave the prayer unless you have thought, "All right, God has heard my prayer, and I truly know this for certain, for that is what *Amen* means."

We never pray this prayer alone, but with all Christendom, and we never have to wonder if this prayer is pleasing to God. Christ gave it to us! And yes, we know that God has heard our prayer when we pray *like this*.

That is really what *Amen* means. And there is no more perfect way to end our study of the Lord's Prayer, the prayer that turns the world upside down, than with *Amen*.

ACKNOWLEDGMENTS

Gratitude is a Christian mandate, and the most honest Christians are the most grateful. I am sincerely grateful to the many people who, especially during the writing and preparation of this volume, were of particular help to me.

These would include two cohorts of students who served as interns in my office. They represent the very best a school can hope for: Cheston Pickard, Tyler Kirkpatrick, Zach Carter, Joshua Easter, Troy Solava, Mitchell Holley, Ryan Modisette, Cory Higdon, Bruno Sanchez, David Lee, and Ryan Loague.

Jon Swan, my personal librarian, is always an incredible help. I deeply appreciate him, and I am thankful for his superb organizational skills and insights.

Tom Hellams and Jon Austin make the trains run on time in my office and they are colleagues for whom I am very thankful. Colin Smothers, producer of *The Briefing* during this period, was always ready to offer additional insight and reflection.

Above all others on the team, I want to thank Sam

Emadi—now Sam Emadi, PhD—for his skill and commitment as Director of Research in my office. His keen mind and eager heart are great gifts to us all, but I am particularly in his debt.

The editorial staff at Thomas Nelson, led by Webb Younce, are wonderful professionals whose care for authors and expertise in publishing are great gifts.

Finally, I want to thank my wife, Mary, who has never failed to be anything but wise, loving, supportive, encouraging, loving, energizing, and caring, not only for this project and everything else I have done, but of me. Saying thank you is not enough, but it is at least a good place to start.

Gratitude at the start, gratitude at the end, and gratitude at every point along the way. Thank you, dear reader, for sharing this gratitude with me.

NOTES

Introduction

1. Gary Millar, *Calling on the Name of the Lord: A Biblical Theology of Prayer*, New Studies in Biblical Theology, ed. D. A. Carson (Downers Grove, IL: InterVarsity Press/Apollos, 2016), 231.

2. Martin Luther, "A Simple Way to Pray, to Master Peter the Barber," in *Luther's Spirituality*, eds. Philip D. W. Krey and Peter D. S. Krey, Library of Christian Classics (New York: Paulist Press, 2007), 222.

3. Ibid.

Chapter 1: The Lord's Prayer

1. Roger Scruton, *The Aesthetics of Music* (Oxford, UK: Oxford University Press, 1999), 460.

Chapter 2: And When You Pray

1. For instance, a recent Pew Research Center survey revealed that one-quarter of self-identified Christians admit to only praying once a week or

even once a month. Further than that, almost 10 percent indicated that they seldom or never pray. See http://www.pewforum.org/2015/11/03/chapter-2-religious-practices-and-experiences/#private-devotions.

2. This idea is defended and beautifully explained in John Piper, *God Is the Gospel: Meditations on God's Love as the Gift of Himself* (Wheaton, IL: Crossway, 2011).

Chapter 3: Hallowing the Father's Name

1. "The 2000 Baptist Faith and Message," Southern Baptist Convention, accessed July 23, 2017, http://www.sbc.net/bfm2000/bfm2000.asp.

2. Millar, *Calling on the Name of the Lord*, 29.

3. Carl F. H. Henry, *God, Revelation, and Authority*, vol. 3, *God Who Speaks and Shows* (Wheaton, IL: Crossway, 1999), 405.

4. Herman Bavinck, *Reformed Dogmatics* (Grand Rapids: Baker, 2004), 97–99.

5. J. I. Packer, *Knowing God* (Downer's Grove, IL: InterVarsity Press, 1993), 28–29.

Chapter 4: Your Kingdom Come

1. See, for instance, George Eldon Ladd, *The Gospel of the Kingdom* (Grand Rapids: Eerdmans, 1959).

2. Graeme Goldsworthy, *According to Plan: The Unfolding Revelation of God in the Bible* (Downer's Grove, IL: InterVarsity Press, 1991).

3. Phil Ryken, *The Prayer of Our Lord* (Wheaton, IL: Crossway, 2002), 39.

4. J. I. Packer, *Praying the Lord's Prayer* (Wheaton, IL: Crossway, 2007), 57–58.
5. George A. Buttrick, *So We Believe So We Pray* (New York: Abingdon-Cokesbury Press, 1951), 155.

Chapter 5: Give Us This Day

1. John Calvin, *The Institutes of the Christian Religion*, vol. 1 (Philadelphia: Nicklin, 1816), 46.
2. J. I. Packer, *Praying the Lord's Prayer* (Wheaton, IL: Crossway, 2007), 73.
3. Helmut Thielicke, *Our Heavenly Father: Sermons on the Lord's Prayer* (New York: Harper & Row, 1960), 77–89.

Chapter 6: Forgive Us Our Debts

1. Richard Sibbes, *The Bruised Reed* (Zeeland, MI: Reformed Church Publications, 2015), 16.

Chapter 7: Lead Us Not into Temptation

1. C. S. Lewis, *The Screwtape Letters* (London: HarperCollins, 1942), ix.
2. *Soren Kierkegaard's Journals & Papers*, eds. Howard V. Hong and Edna H. Hong, vol. 1, A–E (Bloomington, IN: Indiana University Press, 1967), 90.

Epilogue

1. Packer, *Praying the Lord's Prayer*, 106.
2. Ibid.